TABLE OF CONTENTS

STUDY SUGGESTIONS

Thank you for choosing this study to help you dig into God's Word. We are so passionate about women getting into Scripture, and we are praying that this study will be a tool to help you do that. Here are a few tips to help you get the most from this study:

• Before you begin, take time to look into the context of the book. Find out who wrote it and learn about the cultural climate it was written in, as well as where it fits on the biblical timeline. Then take time to read through the entire book of the Bible we are studying if you are able. This will help you to get the big picture of the book and will aid in comprehension, interpretation, and application.

• Start your study time with prayer. Ask God to help you understand what you are reading and allow it to transform you (Psalm 119:18).

• Look into the context of the book as well as the specific passage.

• Before reading what is written in the study, read the assigned passage! Repetitive reading is one of the best ways to study God's Word. Read it several times, if you are able, before going on to the study. Read in several translations if you find it helpful.

• As you read the text, mark down observations and questions. Write down things that stand out to you, things that you notice, or things that you don't understand. Look up important words in a dictionary or interlinear Bible.

• Look for things like verbs, commands, and references to God. Notice key terms and themes throughout the passage.

• After you have worked through the text, read what is written in the study. Take time to look up any cross-references mentioned as you study.

ARISE

A study on the book of *Nehemiah*

by
KRISTIN SCHMUCKER

STUDY CONTRIBUTORS

Designer:
MICHELE YATES

Assistant Designer:
KATIE LINSTRUM

Editor:
MELISSA DENNIS

www.thedailygraceco.com

• Then work through the questions provided in the book. Read and answer them prayerfully.

• Paraphrase or summarize the passage, or even just one verse from the passage. Putting it into your own words helps you to slow down and think through every word.

• Focus your heart on the character of God that you have seen in this passage. What do you learn about God from the passage you have studied? Adore Him and praise Him for who He is.

• Think and pray through application and how this passage should change you. Get specific with yourself. Resist the urge to apply the passage to others. Do you have sin to confess? How should this passage impact your attitude toward people or circumstances? Does the passage command you to do something? Do you need to trust Him for something in your life? How does the truth of the gospel impact your everyday life?

• We recommend you have a Bible, pen, highlighters, and journal as you work through this study. We recommend that ballpoint pens instead of gel pens be used in the study book to prevent smearing. Here are several other optional resources that you may find helpful as you study:

• www.blueletterbible.org This free website is a great resource for digging deeper. You can find translation comparison, an interlinear option to look at words in the original languages, Bible dictionaries, and even commentary.

• A Dictionary. If looking up words in the Hebrew and Greek feels intimidating, look up words in English. Often times we assume we know the meaning of a word, but looking it up and seeing its definition can help us understand a passage better.

• A double-spaced copy of the text. You can use a website like www.biblegateway.com to copy the text of a passage and print out a double-spaced copy to be able to mark on easily. Circle, underline, highlight, draw arrows, and mark in any way you would like to help you dig deeper and work through a passage.

NEHEMIAH AND JESUS

Nehemiah wept over Jerusalem
NEHEMIAH 1:4

Jesus wept over Jerusalem
LUKE 19:41

Nehemiah was sent by the king
NEHEMIAH 2:8

Jesus was sent by the Father
JOHN 6:38

Nehemiah left the palace to
rescue the people
NEHEMIAH 1

Jesus left heaven to
rescue His people
JOHN 3:16-17

Nehemiah called others to
follow him
NEHEMIAH 2:18

Jesus called his disciples to
follow Him
MATTHEW 4:18-22

Nehemiah was a man of
constant prayer

Jesus prayed throughout
His ministry

Nehemiah had enemies that plotted against him
NEHEMIAH 4:1-7

Jesus' enemies plotted against Him
MATTHEW 27

Nehemiah was accused
NEHEMIAH 6:6-7

Jesus was accused
MATTHEW 26:60-61

Nehemiah finished the work God had called him to do
NEHEMIAH 6:15

Jesus cried "it is finished" as He finished the work God had called Him to do
JOHN 19:28-30

Nehemiah brought the renewal of the old covenant
NEHEMIAH 9-10

Jesus brought the new covenant
HEBREWS 9:15, HEBREWS 7:22

Nehemiah cleansed the temple
NEHEMIAH 13:8-9

Jesus cleansed the temple
MARK 11:15-19, MATTHEW 21:12-13

NEHEMIAH 1:4–11a

[4] *When I heard these words, I sat down and wept. I mourned for a number of days, fasting and praying before the God of the heavens.*

[5] *I said, LORD, the God of the heavens, the great and awe-inspiring God who keeps his gracious covenant with those who love him and keep his commands,*

> [6] *let your eyes be open and your ears be attentive to hear your servant's prayer that I now pray to you day and night for your servants, the Israelites. I confess the sins we have committed against you. Both I and my father's family have sinned.*

[7] *We have acted corruptly toward you and have not kept the commands, statutes, and ordinances you gave your servant Moses.*

[8] *Please remember what you commanded your servant Moses: "If you are unfaithful, I will scatter you among the peoples.*

[9] *But if you return to me and carefully observe my commands, even though your exiles were banished to the farthest horizon, I will gather them from there and bring them to the place where I chose to have my name dwell."*

[10] *They are your servants and your people. You redeemed them by your great power and strong hand.*

[11] *Please, Lord, let your ear be attentive to the prayer of your servant and to that of your servants who delight to revere your name. Give your servant success today, and grant him compassion in the presence of this man.*

NEHEMIAH 2:4

Then the king asked me, "What is your request?" So I prayed to the God of the heavens

NEHEMIAH 4:4–5

[4] *Listen, our God, for we are despised. Make their insults return on their own heads and let them be taken as plunder to a land of captivity.*

[5] *Do not cover their guilt or let their sin be erased from your sight, because they have angered the builders.*

NEHEMIAH 5:19

Remember me favorably, my God, for all that I have done for this people.

NEHEMIAH 6:9

For they were all trying to intimidate us, saying, "They will drop their hands from the work, and it will never be finished." But now, my God, strengthen my hands.

NEHEMIAH 6:14

My God, remember Tobiah and Sanballat for what they have done, and also the prophetess Noadiah and the other prophets who wanted to intimidate me.

NEHEMIAH 9:5–38

⁵ Then the Levites—Jeshua, Kadmiel, Bani, Hashabneiah, Sherebiah, Hodiah, Shebaniah, and Petha-hiah—said, "Stand up. Blessed be the LORD your God from everlasting to everlasting." Blessed be your glorious name, and may it be exalted above all blessing and praise.

⁶ You, LORD, are the only God. You created the heavens, the highest heavens with all their stars, the earth and all that is on it, the seas and all that is in them. You give life to all of them, and all the stars of heaven worship you. ⁷ You, the LORD, are the God who chose Abram and brought him out of Ur of the Chaldeans, and changed his name to Abraham. ⁸ You found his heart faithful in your sight, and made a covenant with him to give the land of the Canaanites, Hethites, Amorites, Perizzites, Jebusites, and Girgashites—to give it to his descendants. You have fulfilled your promise, for you are righteous.

⁹ You saw the oppression of our ancestors in Egypt and heard their cry at the Red Sea. ¹⁰ You performed signs and wonders against Pharaoh, all his officials, and all the people of his land, for you knew how arrogantly they treated our ancestors. You made a name for yourself that endures to this day. ¹¹ You divided the sea before them, and they crossed through it on dry ground. You hurled their pursuers into the depths like a stone into raging water. ¹² You led them with a pillar of cloud by day, and with a pillar of fire by night, to illuminate the way they should go.

continued on next page

¹³ *You came down on Mount Sinai, and spoke to them from heaven. You gave them impartial ordinances, reliable instructions, and good statutes and commands.* ¹⁴ *You revealed your holy Sabbath to them, and gave them commands, statutes, and instruction through your servant Moses.* ¹⁵ *You provided bread from heaven for their hunger; you brought them water from the rock for their thirst. You told them to go in and possess the land you had sworn to give them.*

¹⁶ *But our ancestors acted arrogantly; they became stiff-necked and did not listen to your commands.* ¹⁷ *They refused to listen and did not remember your wonders you performed among them. They became stiff-necked and appointed a leader to return to their slavery in Egypt. But you are a forgiving God, gracious and compassionate, slow to anger and abounding in faithful love, and you did not abandon them.*

¹⁸ *Even after they had cast an image of a calf for themselves and said, "This is your god who brought you out of Egypt," and they had committed terrible blasphemies,* ¹⁹ *you did not abandon them in the wilderness because of your great compassion. During the day the pillar of cloud never turned away from them, guiding them on their journey. And during the night the pillar of fire illuminated the way they should go.*

²⁰ *You sent your good Spirit to instruct them. You did not withhold your manna from their mouths, and you gave them water for their thirst.* ²¹ *You provided for them in the wilderness forty years, and they lacked nothing. Their clothes did not wear out, and their feet did not swell.* ²² *You gave them kingdoms and peoples and established boundaries for them. They took possession of the land of King Sihon of Heshbon and of the land of King Og of Bashan.* ²³ *You multiplied their descendants like the stars of the sky and brought them to the land you told their ancestors to go in and possess.* ²⁴ *So their descendants went in and possessed the land: You subdued the Canaanites who inhabited the land before them and handed their kings and the surrounding peoples over to them, to do as they pleased with them.* ²⁵ *They captured fortified cities and fertile land and took possession of well-supplied houses, cisterns cut out of rock, vineyards, olive groves, and fruit trees in abundance. They ate, were filled, became prosperous, and delighted in your great goodness.*

²⁶ *But they were disobedient and rebelled against you. They flung your law behind their backs and killed your prophets who warned them in order to turn them back to you. They committed terrible blasphemies.* ²⁷ *So you handed them over to their enemies, who oppressed them. In their time of distress, they cried out to you, and you heard from heaven. In your abundant compassion you gave them deliverers, who rescued them from the power of their enemies.*

²⁸ *But as soon as they had relief, they again did what was evil in your sight. So you abandoned them to the power of their enemies, who dominated them. When they cried out to you again, you heard from heaven and rescued them many times in your compassion.* ²⁹ *You warned them to turn back to your law, but they acted arrogantly and would not obey your commands. They sinned against your ordinances, which a person will live by if he does them. They stubbornly resisted, stiffened their necks, and would not obey.* ³⁰ *You were*

patient with them for many years, and your Spirit warned them through your prophets, but they would not listen. Therefore, you handed them over to the surrounding peoples.

31 However, in your abundant compassion, you did not destroy them or abandon them, for you are a gracious and compassionate God.

32 So now, our God—the great, mighty, and awe-inspiring God who keeps his gracious covenant—do not view lightly all the hardships that have afflicted us, our kings and leaders, our priests and prophets, our ancestors and all your people, from the days of the Assyrian kings until today. 33 You are righteous concerning all that has happened to us, because you have acted faithfully, while we have acted wickedly.

34 Our kings, leaders, priests, and ancestors did not obey your law or listen to your commands and warnings you gave them. 35 When they were in their kingdom, with your abundant goodness that you gave them, and in the spacious and fertile land you set before them, they would not serve you or turn from their wicked ways.

36 Here we are today, slaves in the land you gave our ancestors so that they could enjoy its fruit and its goodness. Here we are—slaves in it! 37 Its abundant harvest goes to the kings you have set over us, because of our sins. They rule over our bodies and our livestock as they please. We are in great distress.

38 In view of all this, we are making a binding agreement in writing on a sealed document containing the names of our leaders, Levites, and priests.

NEHEMIAH 13:14

Remember me for this, my God, and don't erase the deeds of faithful love I have done for the house of my God and for its services.

NEHEMIAH 13:22

Then I instructed the Levites to purify themselves and guard the city gates in order to keep the Sabbath day holy. Remember me for this also, my God, and look on me with compassion according to the abundance of your faithful love.

NEHEMIAH 13:29

Remember them, my God, for defiling the priesthood as well as the covenant of the priesthood and the Levites.

NEHEMIAH AND OUR STORY

WEEK ONE

DAY ONE

READ THE ENTIRE BOOK OF NEHEMIAH

Near the center of our Bible is a short book of only thirteen chapters, and yet the message of Nehemiah is a timeless retelling of a faithful God and His people. Though Nehemiah is found near the center of our English Bible, it belongs at the end of the Old Testament by chronology. The book is a companion of sorts to the book of Ezra that comes before it. Throughout much of the book is the first person account of Nehemiah. The author (or at least editor) of the book is generally considered by scholars to be Ezra.

The story of Nehemiah is an account that took place in 445 BC, about 141 years after the destruction of Jerusalem during the Babylonian captivity. The book opens in Susa which was the winter home of the Persian kings. Nehemiah was a Jew born during the exile, and the text tells us that he had rose to a prominent position of leadership in the court of Artaxerxes. As the cupbearer to the king, he would have been a trusted advisor and held responsible for testing the king's wine to make sure that no one was trying to poison him. He was likely equivalent to the king's chief of staff.

The book of Nehemiah has several themes that surface throughout it. We see God sovereignly working through faithful people to bring about the plan of redemption. Our attention is also drawn to themes of covenant, the relationship of prayer and action, and leadership. The city of Jerusalem was a mess at the start of the book, but we will see the difference that one person can make who is passionate about God's kingdom. The seemingly impossible task of rebuilding the wall would be completed in just 52 days under the faithful leadership of Nehemiah. Nehemiah would work to try to restore the kingdom, but we also see glimpses of God's plan that was so much greater than an earthly and physical kingdom. The true King was coming.

So why should we study the book of Nehemiah? What does it have to do with us? It is helpful for us as we begin this study to do a quick recap of the history of Israel. It all began in the garden when God created the first man and woman. Things quickly took an unfortunate turn when Adam and Eve sinned. Though their sin brought the consequence of death, God would also give a promise that a Redeemer was coming. They didn't know when and they didn't know how, but they knew that hope was coming. God would make a covenant with Abraham that would change everything. Abraham would lead a called out nation that would one day birth a Messiah who would bring hope to the entire world (Genesis 12:1-3). Eventually the nation of Israel would find themselves in captivity in Egypt, but God would deliver them from that and would make a covenant with Moses that He would be their God and that there would be great blessing for obedience (Exodus 19:3-6). The history of Israel in the Old Testament may seem like a rollercoaster ride of judges and kings, obedience and blessing, and idolatry and consequences, but through it all God was ever faithful. To David, He would make a great promise that a king would come through David's line that would be unlike any other king (2 Samuel 7:8-16). Sadly, though God had made covenants of promise with His people, they rebelled against His gracious hand (2 Kings 17:5-15). God's people would go into captivity as a result of their sin (2 Chronicles 36:15-20). The nation that had been promised blessing for obedience had chosen rebellion and captivity instead. Yet even in the midst of a destroyed city and God's people carried off to exile, God was faithful. He promised that a remnant would return. God was even telling His sovereign plan to the prophets generations before it would take place, and Isaiah 44-45 records what God spoke to the prophet Isaiah.

So the book of Nehemiah opens with great need. But more importantly there is a great God who has faithfully pursued His people from the garden. This is the story of our God and His people, and that means that this is our story as well. Galatians 3:7-9 and verses 28-29 show us the beautiful truth that as believers in Christ we have been made a part of God's family. We are His people, and this is our history.

So open your Bible and study the book of Nehemiah with us. And as you look at the life of Nehemiah, let your heart be pointed to the One that Nehemiah foreshadowed. Let your gaze be lifted to Jesus.

1 From the introduction and your reading of the book of Nehemiah, write down everything that you know about who Nehemiah was.

2 What did you observe about God in the book of Nehemiah?

3 What do you think are the biggest takeaways from the book of Nehemiah?

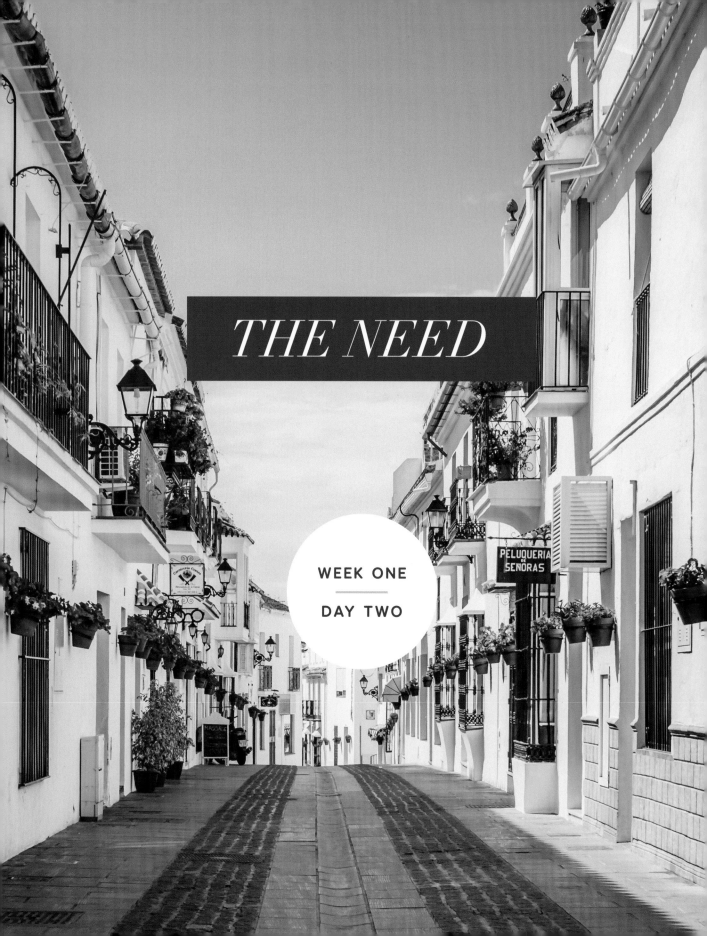

THE NEED

WEEK ONE

DAY TWO

NEHEMIAH 1:1-4

It was about thirteen years after Ezra had led a mission to rebuild the temple that we see Hanani bring the message of the condition of Jerusalem to Nehemiah. Nehemiah asks for a status update on the promised land, specifically the city of Jerusalem and the exiles that had returned from captivity. The news was not good. Hanani told of broken-down walls and people in trouble and shame. It is hard for us to fully understand this concept of a city wall because it is foreign to us. What was at stake here? The wall was the security of the city, so without it, Jerusalem was left open to attack from every side. This is what kept the nation separate and secure from the surrounding nations. Without it, the nation would blend into the culture around them, face military opposition, and likely cease to exist. But Nehemiah's concern was much deeper than just patriotism to his homeland. Nehemiah was concerned for God's people and for the glory of God's name. Nehemiah knew that God had promised a Messiah that would come from Israel. A Deliverer was promised that would make right all that had been made wrong by sin. But if there was no Israel, there would be no Messiah. Nehemiah felt the weight of that truth, and his heart was moved to action. Nehemiah recognized that God was writing a story of redemption through His people, and he was willing to play his part in this grand narrative. Nehemiah was willing to do his part to pave the way for the true Restorer.

Nehemiah heard the news, and he got to work. He was moved with loving compassion that compelled him to do something. But you might be surprised to find that the first thing that he did was to pray for four months. In our minds, prayer is often a last resort or something extra to do. But to Nehemiah it was his first response and the most important thing that could be done. Nehemiah recognized that God was the only one that could restore what had been broken in Jerusalem. If the walls were going to rise, it was going to be because God was at work. Prayer was Nehemiah's first priority, and the work of rebuilding began with coming to God in prayer. Prayer was the first response of

Nehemiah in a time of trouble, but prayer will never be our first response in a time of trouble if it has not first become a daily habit and rhythm in our lives. Sometimes the greatest work that we can do is to get on our knees. Do not be afraid to get still before the Lord before getting up and doing the work. Some may use prayer as an excuse for why they are not moved to action, but that was not Nehemiah. His time in prayer spurred him on to greater action. Prayer is the necessary step to motivate our hearts and energize our work for God.

As we look at the life of Nehemiah, we can't help but see how Nehemiah points ahead to One who is even greater. Nehemiah points us forward to Jesus. Jesus is moved with compassion for us. He is our Intercessor. In John 17, we get a sweet glimpse at the heart of God for His people as Jesus intercedes for His disciples and those like us that would follow Him after His time on earth. Jesus is the One that brings restoration from our ruin. He is the Compassionate Leader. He is the Rebuilder of all that is broken. He is the Restorer. He is the Savior.

So our response to the book of Nehemiah is not simply to desire to be like Nehemiah, but to desire for God to transform us into the image of the One that Nehemiah pointed to. Instead of standing in awe of the faith of Nehemiah, we turn our gaze to the One that he placed his faith in.

1 Describe Nehemiah's response to the problem. What is your typical response to a problem?

2 How does a knowledge of what God is doing in redemptive history shift our perspective for the situations we face each day? How might this have shifted Nehemiah's perspective? How can it change ours?

3 How does Nehemiah point to Jesus?

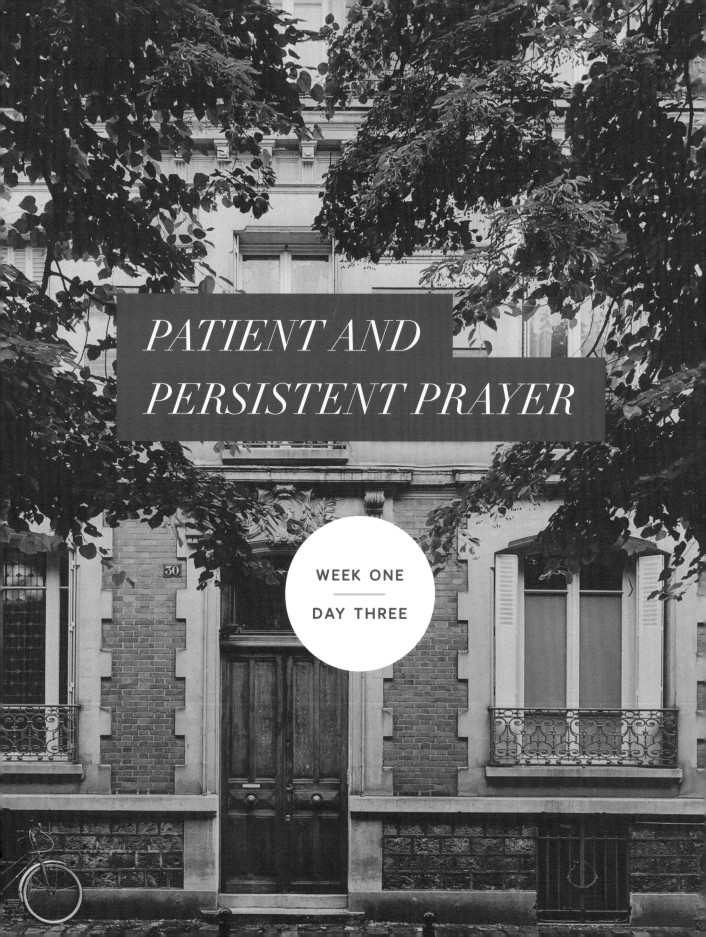

PATIENT AND PERSISTENT PRAYER

WEEK ONE

DAY THREE

NEHEMIAH 1:4-11

Nehemiah was now aware of the situation, and his response is to turn to God in prayer. Nehemiah was a man of God, and we see that he was also a man of prayer. The habit of prayer was likely something that had been cultivated in his life long before this situation. This is a reminder to us of the need for cultivating spiritual disciplines in our lives, so that when difficulty comes, we will be equipped to turn to God instead of relying on our own strength.

In the prayer of Nehemiah, we see him praying Scripture. He is coming to God in adoration. Adoration reminds us of who God is. It worships while it draws us near to Him. Adoration resets our perspective. So often we come to prayer without even realizing that we are focused on ourselves and what we can get from God. Adoration shifts our perspective and reminds us that above all, we want God Himself. Nehemiah's prayer is a beautiful example for us of how we should pray. This prayer is overflowing with quotes or references to Scripture (Deuteronomy 4:25-31, Leviticus 26:40). Nehemiah found strength in the Word of God. God's Word is where we should find comfort and strength as well. When we do not know what to pray, we can pray God's Word back to Him. We can come asking Him to keep His promises and be to us what we know that He is. Prayer should be rooted in God's Word. Kathy Keller said, "Praying Scripture-filled prayers radically reorients us away from our self-absorption, giving us perspective, removing our worry and our panic, by humbling us before God." God's Word is living and powerful. Reading and praying Scripture is transformative to our hearts.

Nehemiah's prayer began with adoration and then moves into confession. Repentance and confession are not topics that we often gravitate toward in our culture. We don't like to think about our sin, but it is our sin and need that point us to the gospel and our great need for our Savior. It is also interesting to note that Nehemiah did not shift the blame.

As a faithful servant of God, he does not blame others for the sin of the nation. He groups himself into those that had been unfaithful and had sinned. Though Nehemiah may not have sinned in the same ways as some of the rest of the nation, he was humble and aware that he also needed God's mercy and grace. After worshiping, adoring, and confessing, Nehemiah reminds God of His promises and covenants and petitions God to act for His people. Our God is a covenant-keeping God. He is true to His promises. Though Israel had wandered far from God and had faced the consequences of their disobedience, Nehemiah knew that God would be faithful to His people. So he prayed, and he pleaded for God to act.

We read this account in our Bibles and read seamlessly through the end of chapter 1 into chapter 2 without realizing that the time that had elapsed was about four months. Nehemiah did not pray once and go on with his life. He dedicated himself to prayer for months. Prayer should be patient and persistent and rooted in trust that God will be faithful. This is what Nehemiah did. He continued in prayer. The season of prayer is often one of waiting and struggle. We don't often like waiting and struggle, which is probably one of the main reasons that we do not pray. We want to pray and have an answer the same day. And though God often does answer prayers within moments or hours, so often the answer may not be revealed for days and months—or even years. Nehemiah did not know how this story would turn out, yet he prayed. He did not know what the answer would be, yet he prayed. And this is why we must know God's Word and trust in the faithfulness and sovereign plan of our God. Because the answer to our prayers may not come in the moment or the way that we expect, but it will come. He will hear. He will answer. He will work on our behalf. For now, we will pray, we will trust, and we will wait.

"PRAYER SHOULD BE PATIENT AND PERSISTENT AND ROOTED IN TRUST THAT GOD WILL BE FAITHFUL.

1 Read Nehemiah's prayer and identify the different sections of the prayer. Write an outline of the prayer below.

2 What does your outline show you about how we should pray?

3 Prayer is often accompanied by waiting and trusting. Why are these things hard for us? Read Isaiah 40:28–31 and write down what happens while we wait.

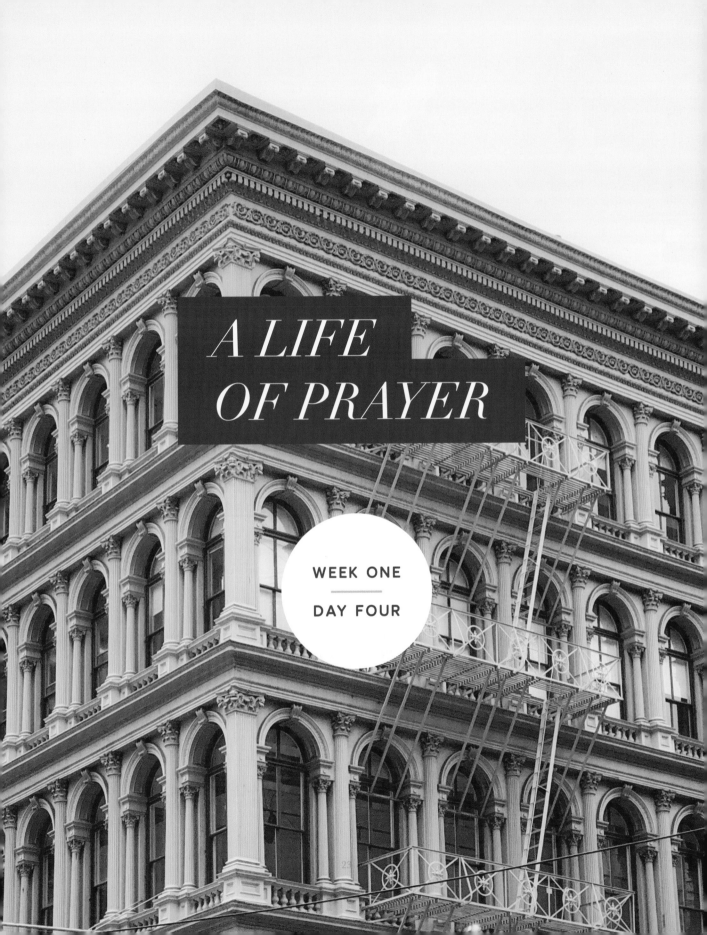

A LIFE OF PRAYER

WEEK ONE

DAY FOUR

NEHEMIAH 2:1-4

If Nehemiah's life were a movie, "four months later..." would pop up on the screen right about now. Nehemiah had been praying for months when we open to chapter 2. It is already evident to us as the reader that Nehemiah was a man of prayer. His life was characterized by both extended prayer time with the Lord, as well as short spontaneous prayers throughout his days. Through Nehemiah's time in prayer, a plan was forming. As Nehemiah prayed for deliverance, God was beginning to shape his heart to see that he would be a key part of that deliverance. As we pray, God shifts our perspective.

At the start of chapter 2, we find Nehemiah coming before King Artaxerxes. It seems to be a typical workday for Nehemiah. We are not told explicitly in the text if Nehemiah came in with a plan that day, or if the weight of the situation was weighing heavily on him and prompting the exchange that we see take place. Nehemiah's sadness caught the king's attention that day. We must note that verse 2 tells us that Nehemiah was afraid. Nehemiah was in a scary position with one of the most powerful men in the world, yet he knew he needed to act. He is the perfect example here of "feel the fear, and do it anyway." Nehemiah was afraid, but he did not let that fear stop him from following where God was leading. Sometimes following God is not the easy path, but we can bring our fear to the One that is stronger than any situation that we will face. We can lay our fear at the feet of Jesus and go forward in His strength.

Nehemiah acted that day in anticipation of the faithfulness of God. As we read his story, we can't help but remember the story of Esther who also made a bold request before a Persian king. And just as it was true for Esther, God had put Nehemiah right where he was in a position of great influence, "for such a time as this." God doesn't need us to accomplish His sovereign plan, and yet He graciously uses His people. He invites us into this grand narrative that He is writing and allows us be a part of His story.

After Nehemiah declares his loyalty to the king and explains the situation, we come to the end of verse 4. The king plainly asks Nehemiah what his request is, and now it is the big moment. Nehemiah was just about to make a bold request, but before he requests anything from the king, he requests something from God. In an instant, Nehemiah turns his heart toward heaven and prays. We aren't told exactly what that prayer contained, but I can imagine it may have just been a few words in his heart asking God to help him in this moment.

The short prayer that Nehemiah prayed is evidence of a vibrant prayer life. It shows us that Nehemiah wanted to live in God's presence. He spent both extended time in prayer seeking the Lord and also communed with God throughout his day. He was so dependent on the Lord that a moment that could have been one filled with anxiety was full of prayer instead. Prayer and Bible study are confession of our own weakness and acknowledgement of our need for Him. Nehemiah is a great example of a man that was aware of his need and turned to God for provision. But even greater than the example of Nehemiah is the God of Nehemiah. Our God is a God who cares about our greatest needs and also longs to equip us in moments of decision. God was ready and waiting to answer the prayer that took place in an instant in the heart of His child, and He will certainly do the same for us. Isaiah 65:24 gives us a glimpse at the character of our God who answers before we even call and hears while we are still speaking. Yet He still longs for us to call on Him. Our God desires relationship with us. He longs to have extended time with us which could be similar to what we may call quiet time. He delights in us spending dedicated time in prayer and Bible study. Yet He also wants us to remember how much we need Him and turn to Him all day long, whispering His name all day long.

1 We all face fear. In this passage Nehemiah was afraid, yet he still did what God had called him to do. What is something that is hard for you, and how can you lean on the Lord during those moments?

2 Both dedicated time with the Lord and spontaneous prayer throughout the day are important for a vibrant relationship with God. Which one is more of a struggle for you? How can you seek the Lord more this week?

3 Nehemiah was not crippled by his fear and anxiety, but instead he turned to the Lord and found strength in the Lord to proceed. How can we do the same?

PRAYER, PLANNING, AND THE POWER OF GOD

WEEK ONE

—

DAY FIVE

NEHEMIAH 2:5-8

Yesterday we closed with Nehemiah's spontaneous prayer in the court of the king. Nehemiah's life of prayer had flowed into a single moment when he needed God to show up for him, and we were encouraged to live our lives in God's presence. Now we come to the request of Nehemiah to Artaxerxes, and it is a big one. Though we aren't sure whether Nehemiah had planned to address the king on this day, he certainly had been thinking and planning about how this situation could be fixed. The months of prayer obviously also included time spent thinking through every detail as God began to shape a plan for Nehemiah to rebuild. So when the opportunity presented itself for Nehemiah to make a very bold request, he was prepared. He asked the king to allow him to return to Jerusalem and rebuild the broken-down wall. Nehemiah presented all the carefully thought out details of how long it would take and how it would work, and then he took his request even further by asking the king to send him with letters that would give him safe passage in his travels. The king obliged to Nehemiah's request, and the section ends with a declaration from Nehemiah that the good hand of God was upon him.

These verses are a reminder to us of how our God works. He works sovereignly in every situation. If God can change the heart of a foreign king, He can certainly change the situations that we find ourselves in. Nehemiah had prayed bold prayers and asked for bold things from the king, and God answered those prayers. When we look at this situation, we can't help but see God's hand in every detail. From the boldness and bravery of Nehemiah to the favor of Artaxerxes, the only explanation for these events is that God was at work. We should not be surprised by the sovereign working of our God. Proverbs 21:1 tells us that the king's heart is in the hand of the Lord. God can change the heart of kings, and He can make the impossible possible.

In the end, Nehemiah recognized that these miraculous events were not his own doing, and he attributed this great success to the Lord alone. We work for God's glory and not our own. We serve Him, not to do the things that Christians should do, but as an overflow from a heart of obedience that has been transformed by His grace. We must be aware of our own weakness as we humbly surrender to the Lord, and then as we see Him work we will know that it is *Him*. As we constantly point our hearts back to the gospel and are reminded of our own weakness, we can see all the more His magnificent strength on display in our situations. We bring our humble service, and He transforms it. He doesn't need us, but He chooses us.

The good hand of God is signifying God's gracious power at work. It is this same power of God that is at work in our hearts as believers (Ephesians 1:17-19). Our God is powerful and strong, and His plans are never thwarted as we are reminded in Job 42:1. Nehemiah found favor in the eyes of the king, but it was the King of Kings whose sovereign power and grace were put on display that day.

Nehemiah prayed big, bold prayers, and God gave him even more than he asked for. We can trust that He will do the same for us. He will do abundantly and immeasurably more than we could ever ask or think (Ephesians 3:20). He will be good. That is who He is.

1 How do prayer and planning go together? How do we balance planning and action with seeking the Lord in our decisions?

2 God's plans are never thwarted. Read Job 42:1, Psalm 135:6, Isaiah 46:8–11, 1 Chronicles 29:11–13. How do these verses give you confidence in the Lord?

3 Read Ephesians 3:20 and look at how the power of God in us accomplishes more than we could ever imagine. How does this verse give you confidence for trusting God in your life right now?

> OUR GOD IS POWERFUL
> AND STRONG, AND HIS
> PLANS ARE NEVER THWARTED

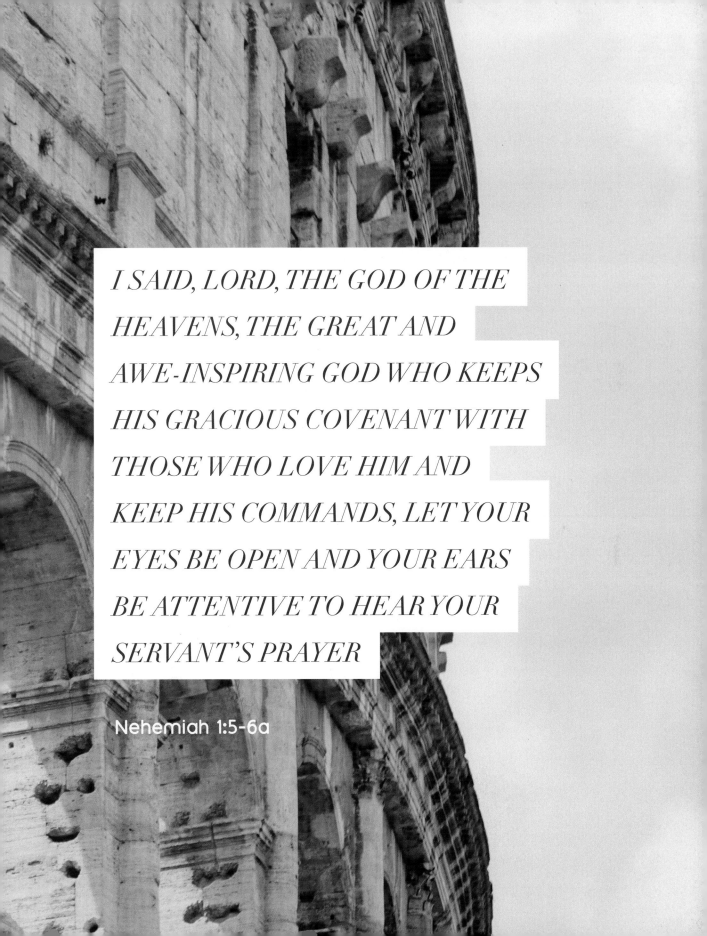

I SAID, LORD, THE GOD OF THE HEAVENS, THE GREAT AND AWE-INSPIRING GOD WHO KEEPS HIS GRACIOUS COVENANT WITH THOSE WHO LOVE HIM AND KEEP HIS COMMANDS, LET YOUR EYES BE OPEN AND YOUR EARS BE ATTENTIVE TO HEAR YOUR SERVANT'S PRAYER

Nehemiah 1:5-6a

WEEK ONE REFLECTION

READ NEHEMIAH 1:1–2:8

Paraphrase the passage from this week.

What did you observe from this week's text about God and His character?

What does the passage teach about the condition of mankind and about yourself?

How does this passage point to the gospel?

How should you respond to this passage? What is the personal application?

What specific action steps can you take this week to apply the passage?

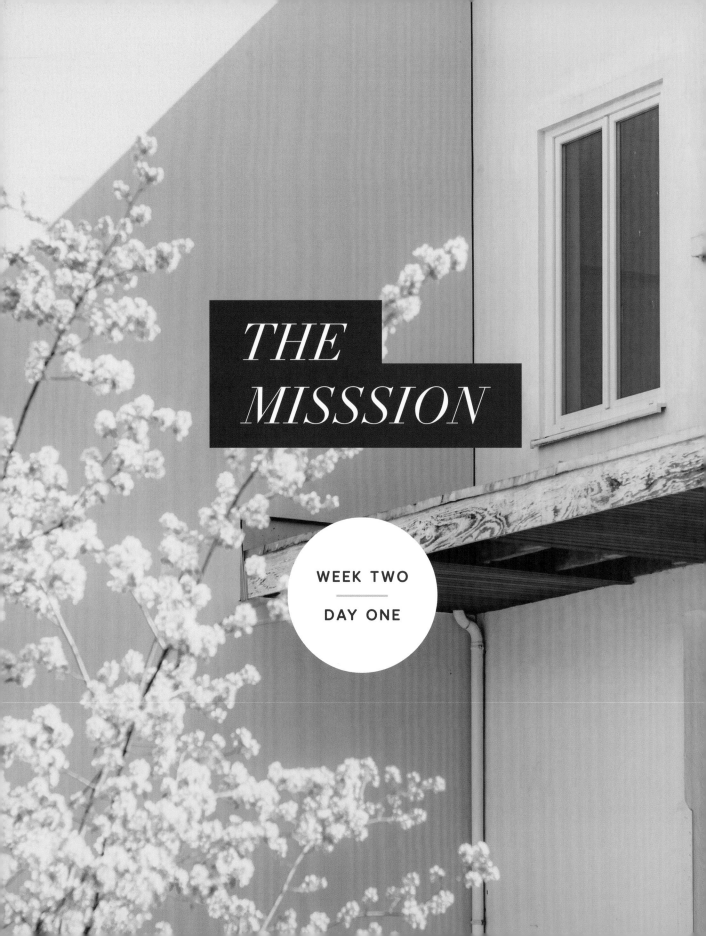

THE MISSSION

WEEK TWO

DAY ONE

NEHEMIAH 2:9-16

Another four months have passed while Nehemiah patiently journeyed to Jerusalem. It had been months since Nehemiah had heard of the great need, and the months had been covered in prayer and planning. Being used by God often begins with prayer and preparation. Patience and waiting are often things that mark our journeys in serving the Lord. We often push against seasons of waiting and preparation, but God uses those seasons to prepare us for the work that He has called us to do.

There was one other thing that Nehemiah faced that we push against in our own lives. *Opposition*. Nehemiah had just arrived in the city when Sanballet and Tobiah showed up in opposition to Nehemiah's plans for rebuilding. Sometimes opposition comes when we are right in the center of God's will. In our minds we often think that if we are faithfully following the Lord we will not have opposition, trials, or suffering. But Nehemiah's story and all of Scripture point us to a far different conclusion. When we are serving the Lord, opposition will come. But in the midst of the struggle, God will be with us. The struggle is real, but so is our God. He is stronger than the strongest enemy. He is greater than anything that may come against us.

God had a very specific task for Nehemiah to do, but He didn't tell him every detail of how to get things done. Nehemiah had to exercise wisdom and discernment in how to proceed. God promises to give wisdom when we call upon Him for it (James 1:5), and from Nehemiah's life thus far, we can be assured that he was in constant prayer over the situation that he was facing. Nehemiah was facing hard and difficult work ahead of him, but he got moving as soon as he arrived in Jerusalem. Verse 12 gives us a bit of insight into what kept Nehemiah focused. In this verse we see that it was God Himself who had put it on Nehemiah's heart to do this work. This is what spurred Nehemiah to action. This is what kept him from giving up even when opposition came. Nehemiah was doing what he was doing because it was what God had called him to do. God calls each of us to do something unique. Nehemiah's task may seem great as we read this account, but his story is full of a lot of prayer, a lot of waiting, and a lot of intense labor. The work was sometimes mundane, but he pressed on because it was what God had called him to do. Colossians 3:23 reminds us that whatever it is that we have to do, we should work for the Lord and not for men. We must shift our gaze from the task we are doing to the One we are doing it for. Mundane tasks are transformed into sacred offerings in His presence.

Nehemiah was coming on to the scene after failed attempts at rebuilding the wall. The task was hard and the people that he would need to help him were discouraged. But instead of being overwhelmed, Nehemiah saw an opportunity to be overwhelmed by God's faithfulness. He didn't know how it would all work out, but he was trusting the One that did. He trusted in faith that God would accomplish the task. What a reminder for us as well. We can trust God to finish the work that He has called us to do. Our task is simply to be faithful right where He has placed us. Whether in grand work or in everyday and mundane tasks, we can work with joy because we are working for Him alone. Nehemiah's strength was not his own—it was the strength that comes from dependence on the One who is strong in us. Jesus is our strength right in the midst of our weakness (2 Corinthians 12:9-10). The gospel shifts our perspective and allows us to see the holy work right where we are.

1 Nehemiah's journey was full of waiting and even opposition. How have you faced these things in your own journey with the Lord? How does Nehemiah's story encourage you?

2 Read James 1:5. Nehemiah needed wisdom in his life, and we need God's wisdom as well. Meditate on James 1:5 and then write a prayer below asking God for wisdom.

3 Read Colossians 3:23. Are you ever tempted to live to please others? How does living for God bring purpose to the mundane? How does it shift our focus?

ARISE

WEEK TWO

DAY TWO

NEHEMIAH 2:17-20

Nehemiah now has the task of not only beginning the work of rebuilding the wall of Jerusalem but also of encouraging the discouraged people to help him do this work. The people had seen failed attempts and were weary. But Nehemiah was a man of God and a leader that could rouse the people to action and excitement. Nehemiah pointed the people to the problem. Not only was the wall broken down, but it was bringing reproach on the people and most of all on the name of God. Nehemiah encouraged them to work for God's glory, not their own. Nehemiah stirred in their hearts a desire for God's kingdom to go forth. Can't you feel the excitement as you read! What a sweet reminder for us to be passionate about building God's kingdom so that we can live out the words that Jesus taught us to pray for God's kingdom to come and His will to be done on earth, just as it is in heaven.

Nehemiah is an example to us of how to lead and encourage others. He didn't call them out for not fixing the problem before he arrived. He did not make himself seem better than them. Nehemiah was well aware of his own need before the Lord which we saw in his prayer in chapter 1. When he spoke of the need, he included himself. He also included himself in the call to build. He would not be standing on the sidelines. He was getting his hands dirty, just like a great leader does.

Nehemiah came to the people, and he told what God had done and was doing in his own life. He told them about the king and the miracle of the king sending him back to Jerusalem. He told them how God's hand was upon him. Something amazing happens when we share our stories. Our stories encourage others to pursue the Lord. It is almost as if Nehemiah is inviting them into the beautiful story that God is writing, and saying, "Don't you want to be a part of this?" The people's response was to echo his call back to him and strengthen their hands for the work that was ahead. They were encouraged and wanted to build for God's name.

Opposition was not far behind the call to build, and Sanballet, Tobiah, and Geshem arrived to try to discourage them from the work that they were beginning. Though these men were the visible opposition, they were not the real enemy. We have an enemy who is always at work to undermine the plans of God and to discourage the people of God. Satan seeks to make God's people doubt His goodness, and his plan has been the same since the garden. The enemy comes to us with lies, and we need to be so grounded in the truth that we can resist the temptation to doubt God's goodness and faithfulness. We must remember that if God is for us, there is no one that can stand against us (Romans 8:31).

Nehemiah reminded the people of who they are. He reminded them that they were God's people. And he let the opposition know as well. The enemy has no claim over the people of God. We need to be reminded of who we are, so that we can stand against our enemy. We can stand firm in our identity as God's people who have been chosen and set apart. *We are His*. We have been called out of darkness and into His light (1 Peter 2:9). We can preach the gospel and the goodness of God back to ourselves when we are tempted to be discouraged. We can look to the cross and be reminded that God has given everything for our good and His glory. And because of all that He has done for us, we must arise. We must arise as His daughters and build. We must arise and fight spiritual battles. We must arise and seek His kingdom. We must arise and proclaim the gospel. We must arise and pursue holiness. We must arise and put our sin to death. We must arise and be who we are.

> THE ENEMY HAS NO CLAIM
> OVER THE PEOPLE OF GOD.

1 How can you lead or encourage others right where God has placed you?

2 What part of your story can you encourage others with? Write down someone you can share what God is doing in your life with this week.

3 We have a real enemy, and he is seeking to make us doubt the Lord and forget who we are. Make two lists. Make one list of who God is and another list of who we are in Christ. How do these lists change our perspective?

REBUILDING TOGETHER

WEEK TWO

DAY THREE

NEHEMIAH 3

A quick look at Nehemiah 3 may make us want to skim through this passage. This building plan of sorts is a list of names and locations of those that worked on the wall, and it seems similar to a genealogy to us. But under the surface of these names and places there is a stronger message and a deeper significance. Chapter 3 helps us see several things about the building of the wall. It helps us to see the unity of this group of people as they worked together on this kingdom work. It shows us how every member of God's family is valuable and given purpose in the work set before us. And it shows us the plan of the great leader Nehemiah and points us to the greater Nehemiah who is Jesus Himself who has come to rebuild all that has been broken in His people.

The wall is divided into 41 sections in chapter 3, and each person or group of people were given a specific assignment to rebuild. Nehemiah had taken care to form a seamless plan that would get the work done quickly and effectively. And each person and group would need to finish the task they had been assigned in order for the work to be completed. If one person did not do what they had been called to do, the work would suffer. When God's people work together, the kingdom of God moves forward. As we read through this list of names and occupations, we find a great variety of people. But we do not find any carpenters or professional wall builders in the list. There were people from every walk of life, but they were just ordinary people. God always uses people that are willing. He is not looking for experts, but willing hearts.

We see priests doing the hard labor usually reserved for others, we see people working on the wall right next to their homes, and we even see a man bringing his daughters to work on the wall which would have been unheard of in this culture. These were ordinary people led by a great leader to serve an extraordinary God. In a very short time the people would accomplish the work that they had tried to do for decades with no success.

Everything changed with a strong leader, a plan, and the dedication to the task at hand.

As we look at the building of the Jerusalem wall, we can't help but be reminded that we are part of a community of faith as well. As believers, we are called to serve the church and build the kingdom here on earth. The church is made up of ordinary people serving the Lord together. And each of us is needed no matter how small our role seems to be. The work of God does not move forward apart from the mobilization of His people and their surrender to do the work that has been entrusted to them. Passages like Ephesians 4:11-13 and Romans 12:3-8 remind us of the work that we have been called to do as the church. We have been entrusted with the building of the church and the proclamation of the gospel. We have been given kingdom work to do. No task is too small or too mundane—every person is needed to accomplish the task at hand.

The people of God built a wall because they had one single focus. So how do we continue on when the building and labor is hard and long? Hebrews 12:3 reminds us to consider Jesus, to look to Jesus. We must fix our gaze on Him. He endured all things for us so that we would be reminded that we can press on because we have Him with us. May we get to work building His kingdom here on earth and proclaiming the truth of the gospel. And in it all, may we with a steadfast heart consider Jesus.

1 What can we learn from the way that the people worked together? How does this encourage us to serve in the church and for the kingdom?

2 In Nehemiah 3:5, we see that there were nobles who would not stoop to serve the Lord. They thought that they were above this difficult work. How was Nehemiah a different kind of leader based on what we have read about him so far? Read Philippians 2:5–11 and write down how Christ was a different kind of leader as well.

3 As we seek to build God's kingdom and serve Him with our lives, we will face struggle and opposition. Read Hebrews 12:1–3. How does considering or remembering what Jesus has done and who He is give us hope and courage for our own journey?

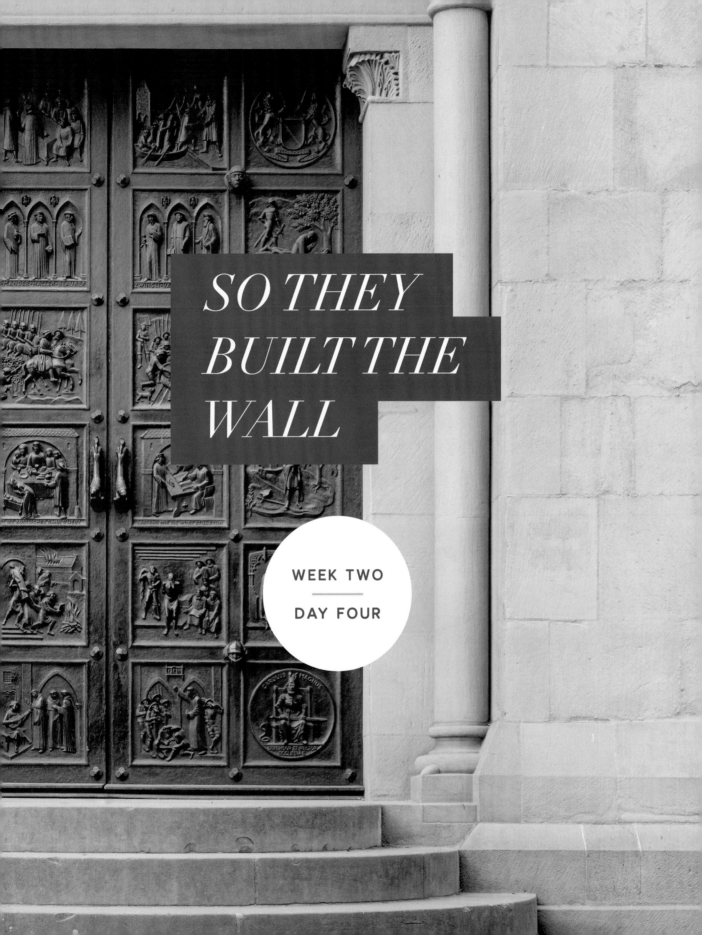

SO THEY BUILT THE WALL

WEEK TWO
—
DAY FOUR

NEHEMIAH 4:1-6

Nehemiah organized the people, and they got to work. Though the task seemed near impossible, Nehemiah was the kind of leader that motivated action and encouraged the people to believe that this task could be accomplished with God's help and a lot of hard work. It wasn't long though before opposition arrived. We see Sanballet and Tobiah return. In chapter 2, we see their jeering at the plan of Nehemiah, and now we see them mocking the work that is being done. They are spewing insults and accusations against the Jews who are hard at work. Have you ever noticed how much easier it is to talk and complain and accuse others than it is to get in and do the hard work? While the Jews were laboring to finish the task that seemed impossible, their enemies were not working, but complaining.

We see that there are a lot of people standing against Nehemiah and the people of God. The rebuilding of the wall would in effect reinstate God's law, and this would mean freedom to worship the Lord, protection for the weak and vulnerable, and a return to the Lord after a long exile. These men were so opposed to this, not just because they were opposed to Israel as a nation, but because they lived at the expense of others. They were part of enemy nations that took advantage of the poor and vulnerable and exploited those in need. The rebuilding of the wall was a declaration that the city of Jerusalem was the city of God and that He would care for His people.

Nehemiah could have gotten angry and decided to stop working and give these men a piece of his mind, but that is not what he does. After looking at Nehemiah's life in the past chapters, we should not be surprised when his first instinct is to go to God in prayer. Nehemiah had built habits of prayer in his life, so when opposition came, he goes straight to the Lord. It is often tempting to take our problems to other people, but the first place that we should run should always be the Lord. Nehemiah comes to the Lord with urgency. He wants the Lord to act on his behalf and on the behalf of the people. Nehemiah prays a bold prayer in these verses. It is the same kind of imprecatory prayer that we often see in the Psalms. Our first instinct may be to be a little shocked at the words that Nehemiah prayed. We may even try to explain it away. Is this a prayer for revenge? Is it sinful to pray this kind of prayer today? Nehemiah was not praying for revenge; he was praying for justice. He was not praying to get back at them for what they had done but for God to be faithful. He was not praying for his own glory, but for the glory of the name of God. Nehemiah knew that by these men deriding God's chosen people, he was insulting the nature and character of God as well. Nehemiah was praying for God to be who He is—holy, just, righteous, and true.

Nehemiah placed the situation in God's almighty hands, and then he got back to work. Immediately following the prayer of Nehemiah are the words, "so they built the wall." Nehemiah and the people did not allow the opposition and distraction to keep them from doing what God had called them to do. We have a very real enemy as well. Our enemy is seeking to distract us and to destroy us. He doesn't want us to finish the work that we have been called to do. He wants us to get apathetic and discouraged. He wants us to give up. Living the life of faith is not always easy, and opposition is sure, but we have a God who is our refuge no matter what schemes the enemy employs. When the enemy attacks, we can follow the example of Nehemiah. We can go to God in prayer and keep working right where God has called us to be.

1 Write down the five attacking questions of Sanballet and the accusation of Tobiah. What accusations does the enemy use in your life?

2 How are you prone to react against opposition? What should be your response?

3 Our enemy is seeking to distract us and destroy us. How does he seek to do this? How do we stand against him? Read Ephesians 6:10–20 for a few ways to stand against our enemy.

WE HAVE A GOD WHO IS OUR
REFUGE NO MATTER WHAT
SCHEMES THE ENEMY EMPLOYS

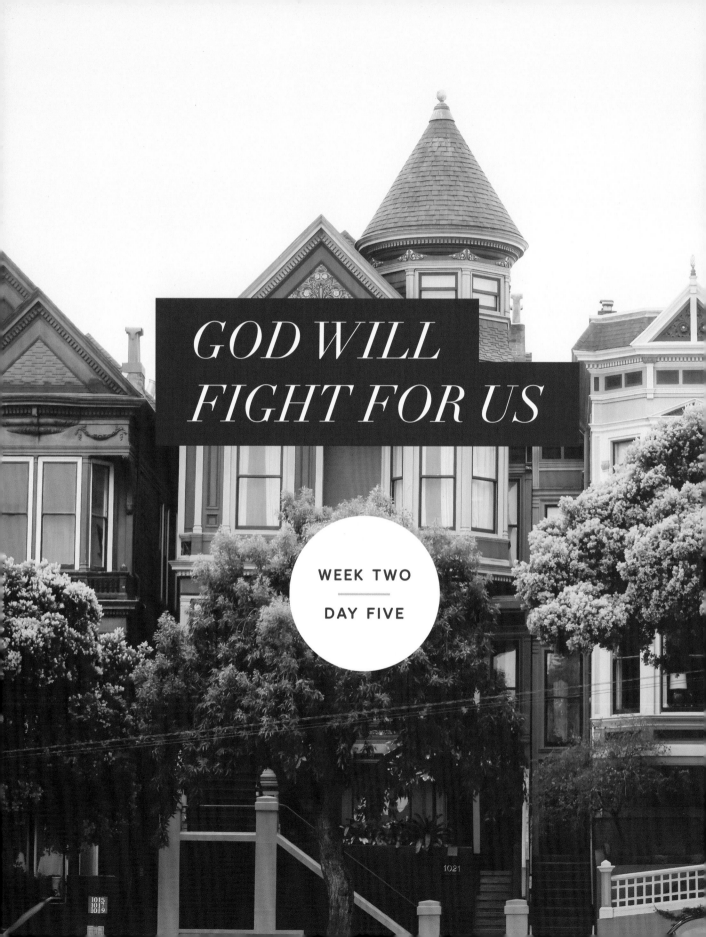

GOD WILL FIGHT FOR US

WEEK TWO

DAY FIVE

NEHEMIAH 4:7-23

When Nehemiah and the children of Israel went right to work despite the opposition that came against them, it only angered the opposition even more. Beginning in verse 7, we see that when the enemies heard that the work was continuing they were enraged. We see multiple nations plotting against God's people and the work that God had called them to do. We already know that Nehemiah is a man of prayer, so we should not be surprised that prayer is his first resort. We also have already seen that Nehemiah is a valiant leader who leads the people to God. This is seen right here as we see not just Nehemiah in prayer, but all the people. Nehemiah was a leader that pointed to the greatest Leader.

Verse 9 is one of the key verses in all of the book of Nehemiah. It is in this verse that we see that the people both prayed and worked. One did not negate the other. The same is true for us. We should never think that we are able to do it on our own and we do not need the Lord's help. We should also never use prayer as an excuse for neglecting the task before us. *Prayer emboldens our action. Prayer fuels our faith. Prayer suffocates our fear.* It is in prayer that we are reminded that though we don't have all the answers, we serve the One that does.

Fear is real, but faith is stronger than fear because God is stronger than anything we could ever be afraid of. The advice of Nehemiah in verse 14 is something that we need to remind ourselves of over and over again. Do not be afraid, instead remember the Lord. Think on who He is. Meditate on His character. Preach the gospel to yourself and remember who He is. There is comfort to be found in the name of Jesus. Remember that He is greater. Remember that He is stronger. Remember that He is working even when we don't understand. Remember that He will not leave you now.

So the people went back to work. With one hand they worked on the wall, and in the other hand they held their weapons. They were ready to fight, but they would let nothing distract them from finishing what God had called them to do. They knew that they may have to enter a battle but that God would fight for them. And they knew that the cause they were fighting for was worth any battle that may come. Nehemiah led them in trusting the Lord. He put into action what the psalmist spoke of in Psalm 20:7. The enemies of God saw a bunch of discouraged former exiles, but God saw His mighty warriors ready to step into battle. What the world saw as a bunch of outcasts, God saw as His chosen people. So the enemies might trust in their horses and weapons and all the things that this world says makes someone great. But God's people trust in the name of the Lord.

The question for us is simple—will you trust the Lord? Will you not allow yourself to be paralyzed by your fear and instead trust that God will fight for you and do the work that He has called you to do? Will you remember the Lord? Will you rest in His Word and trust that the same power that raised Jesus from the dead is now alive and at work in you as God's child? We are called to persevere in the Christian life, but the basis of our perseverance is God and not ourselves. We are weak, but He is strong in us.

1 What is the relationship between prayer and action? How do they work together? Which are you more tempted to depend on?

2 The concept of remembering is one that is seen throughout Scripture. The church today has something specific that we are to do to remember the Lord. Read 1 Corinthians 11:24–26 and write down what it is. Why is it important for us to remember the Lord?

3 We have seen how this passage is a reminder for us to trust the Lord in all things. What is something that you need to trust God in right now?

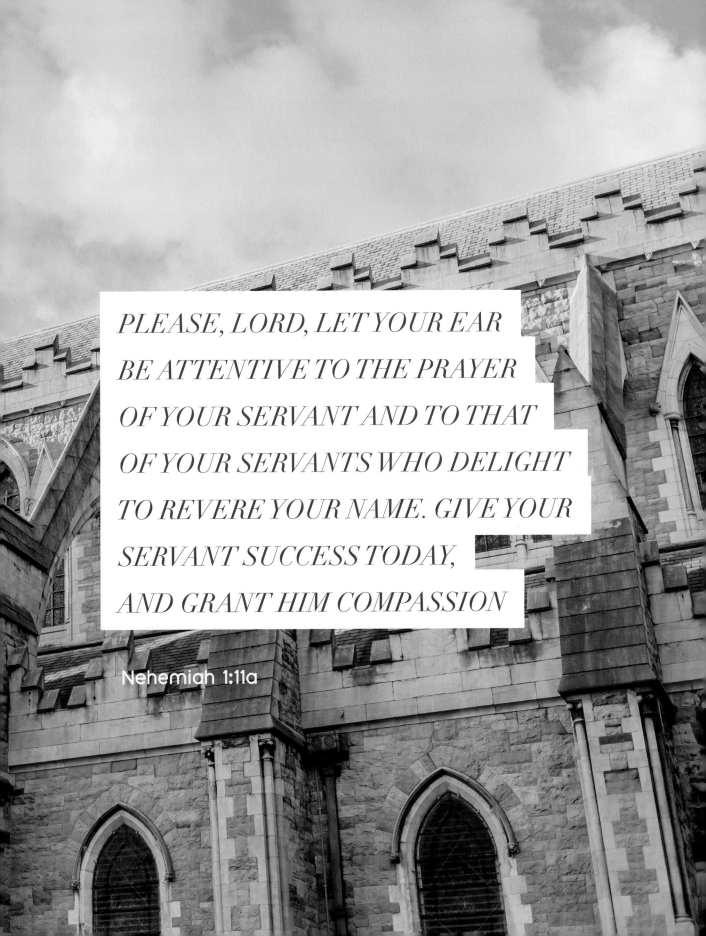

PLEASE, LORD, LET YOUR EAR BE ATTENTIVE TO THE PRAYER OF YOUR SERVANT AND TO THAT OF YOUR SERVANTS WHO DELIGHT TO REVERE YOUR NAME. GIVE YOUR SERVANT SUCCESS TODAY, AND GRANT HIM COMPASSION

Nehemiah 1:11a

WEEK TWO REFLECTION

READ NEHEMIAH 2:9–4:23

Paraphrase the passage from this week.

What did you observe from this week's text about God and His character?

What does the passage teach about the condition of mankind and about yourself?

How does this passage point to the gospel?

How should you respond to this passage? What is the personal application?

What specific action steps can you take this week to apply the passage?

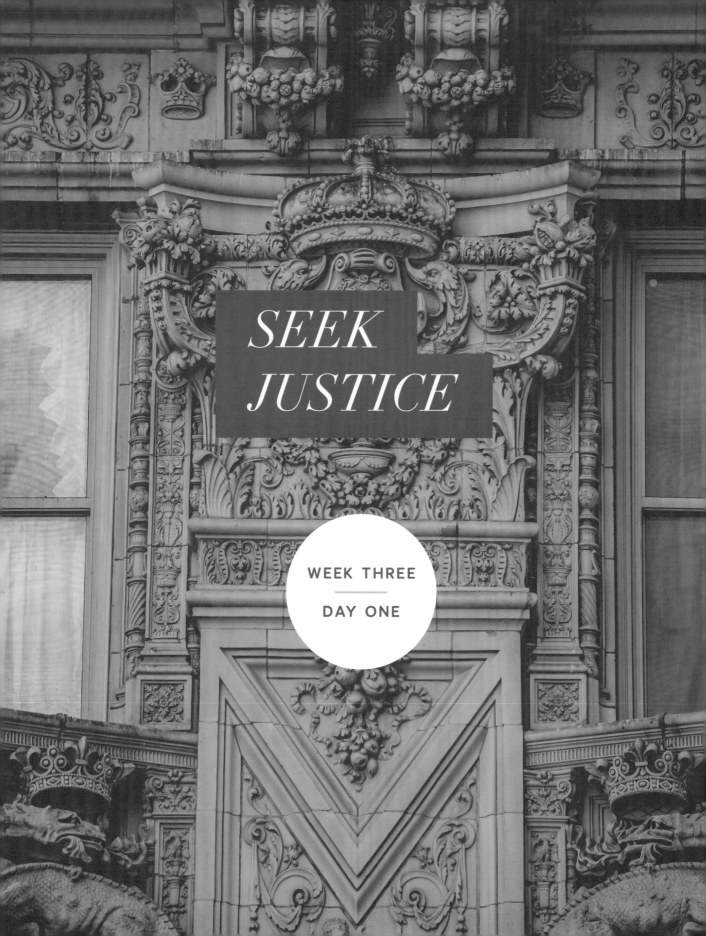

SEEK
JUSTICE

WEEK THREE

DAY ONE

NEHEMIAH 5

Sometimes opposition comes from the enemy outside. But sometimes opposition comes from our own discouragement about the situations around us. At the beginning of chapter 5, we see opposition coming from the discouragement of God's people. Jerusalem was in a bad condition. The poor were being oppressed and charged exorbitant amounts of interest. This was something that was specifically forbidden in the law (Deuteronomy 23:19-20, Leviticus 25:35-42). Some of the people were having to borrow against their homes and fields, and some others were even being forced to have their children become slaves to pay the debts that they owed. The people were upset and rightly so. Their frustration led them to discouragement, and with poor leadership this could have easily stopped the rebuilding of the wall. Thankfully, Nehemiah was a godly man and a great leader, so when he heard of the problem at hand, he took action.

Nehemiah's first response to the news of what was going on was anger. But he then got his emotions under control and spoke truth to his own heart, and then stepped into action. He demanded that those that were taking advantage of the less fortunate stop what they were unlawfully doing. In verse 10, he even admits to his own involvement in the situation. We aren't sure to what extent he was involved, and from his reaction of anger it doesn't seem that he was taking advantage of people like many others, but as a strong leader he did not shrink away from his own involvement in the situation. He had done the same thing when he prayed in chapter 1. He acknowledged his own sin along with the sin of the people. God honors when his people deal with sin. This was the message that Nehemiah was giving as he gave them a clear illustration by shaking out his garment. He was reminding them of what God had spoken to them back in Deuteronomy 28. It was in that chapter that God had clearly shown them that there are blessings for obedience and consequences for disobedience.

The message of this chapter is not that wealth is bad or that there should be a sense of guilt if we have more than someone else does. 1 Samuel 2:7 reminds us that God is the one that grants wealth or withholds it. Having money is not a sin, but the New Testament makes it very clear that loving money is sin (1 Timothy 6:10). Money or anything else that becomes our focus and our sole desire is an idol in our lives, and idolatry is a sin. Possessing money is not a sin, but being possessed by money is. The people in chapter 5 were so controlled by the pursuit of wealth that they would objectify and manipulate other people to get more money.

The last section of the chapter gives us insight into Nehemiah's life. In these verses we learn that he was a man of great wealth but also a man of generosity. As the governor of the land who was sent by Persia, he was entitled to an allowance that would have come from the people. He was entitled to it, and it wouldn't have been wrong for him to take it, but he gave it up so that the work of God would go on without putting any more difficulty on the people. Nehemiah was an extremely wealthy man, and we see in these verses that he entertained over 150 people in his home each day where there was a spread of an ox and six sheep every day for twelve years, and an abundance of wine every ten days. Add that up—it is a lot of oxen and sheep. Nehemiah invited others to his table to eat and drink of the abundance that he had to offer. He used what God had given him to bless others, and this is exactly what we are called to do. We are called to use whatever He has given us, whether that is great wealth or just a small amount to bless those that we come in contact with and to further the kingdom of God.

But Nehemiah only points us to the greater leader that we find in Jesus Christ. It is Jesus who extends compassion for the weak and the exploited. It is Jesus who calls us to repentance. It is Jesus who shares with us His great riches and calls us to freely eat at His table. Because of Jesus, we can pray the same kind of bold prayer that Nehemiah prayed at the end of chapter 5, that God would bless us and remember us. We serve little by little in the ways that He has enabled us to, and then we can humbly and boldly ask for Him to bless the work of our hands.

1 All people are created in God's image, and God hates to see His image-bearers oppressed. Sadly the oppression of people has been a consistent problem in the world. How do we see people oppressed in our generation? How does Micah 6:8 speak into what our responsibility as believers should be to the oppression of others?

2 In what ways does the sin of loving money play out in the lives of people? This sin is seen in both people with a lot and people with a little, how so? How do we guard against the love of money?

3 Why should God's people be characterized by generosity? Generosity is not just limited to money. How can you be generous with what God has blessed you with?

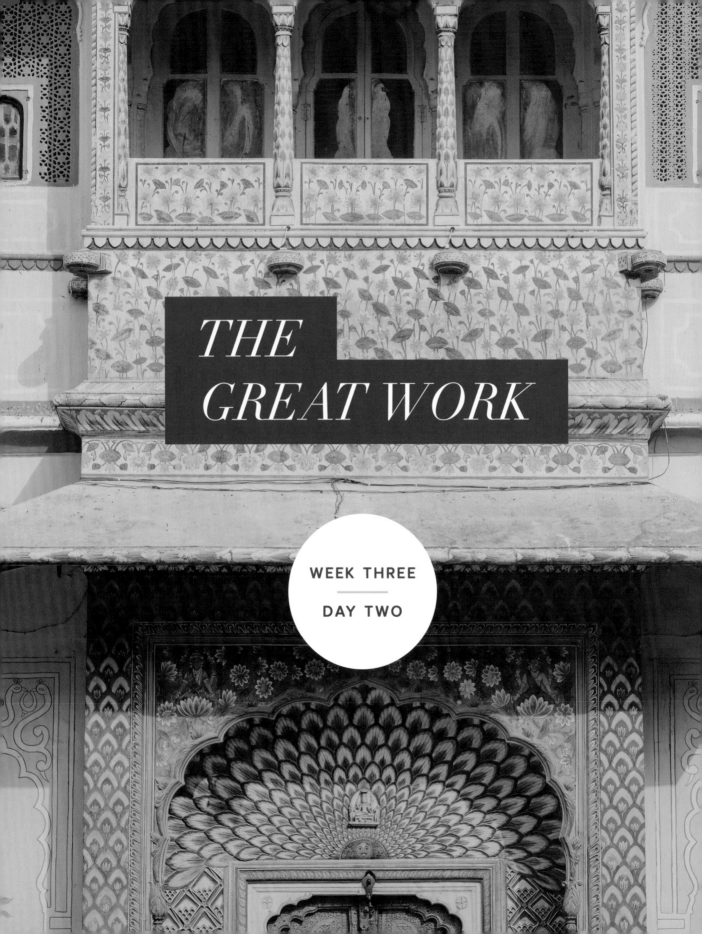

THE GREAT WORK

WEEK THREE

DAY TWO

NEHEMIAH 6:1-14

The opposition has returned again. In chapter 6, Sanballet, Tobiah, and Gesham return and continue to conspire together against Nehemiah and the work of God that he was pursuing. From the start Nehemiah states the great progress that had been made on the wall. Much had been accomplished, but there was still much to be done. When Nehemiah's enemies tried to distract him from the work he was doing, he was not afraid to state that they were his enemies. So often as believers, we neglect to acknowledge that we have an enemy. Satan is roaming this earth seeking to destroy the plan and people of God. He will never succeed at that plan. If our enemy cannot destroy us, he will try to distract us. Nehemiah's enemies had the same plan, but it would not work. They would call for Nehemiah to leave the work and come speak with them. Nehemiah's response was that he would not come down, because he was doing a great work. Nehemiah refused to be distracted from the work that God had called him to do. We have also been given a mission from God. There is kingdom work to do, and we do not have time to be distracted by our enemy.

Nehemiah said that the work he had to do was great. For many in that day, this would have seemed like a joke. The same enemy that seeks to destroy and distract also seeks to discourage. Nehemiah who had once been the cupbearer to the king was now working on a dilapidated old wall. What was so great about that? But the greatness of his task was determined not by what he was doing, but who he was doing it for. The task may have seemed humble and mundane, but it was being done for God alone. Many of us may look at the tasks that we have been called to do and think that they are not as important as some other vocations and callings, but the greatest task that we can do is the one that God has called us to do. For some that will be proclaiming the message of the gospel in a foreign land, and for some it will be teaching some women in our church, or reading the Bible to our children. For some it may be leading great movements for justice, and for others it will be going to work every day to provide for our families, or serving in our singleness, or staying at home with kids. Our life calling is not something mysterious. Our calling is to be faithful right where God has placed us. We are all called to do great things, and the greatest thing we can do is to lift high the name of Jesus in all that we do. No task is too small to bring glory to God (1 Corinthians 10:31). Even the mundane is a great work when it is done for the glory of God and placed in the hands of God. We do our part and then we watch Him use what we have done.

The enemies were spreading lies about Nehemiah wanting to become the king of Judah and that being the reason for the work that was being done. They were wrong that Nehemiah was doing this work out of rebellion or for personal gain. But they weren't wrong that there would be a king in Judah. The King was coming. The work that these men and women would prepare this city for would be a great King that would not come until the record of the Old Testament would close. King Jesus would come to Jerusalem, and He will someday rule over all (Psalm 110:1). Nehemiah's response to the attacks of these men was again to turn to God in prayer. He prayed as he worked and asked God to strengthen his hands for the task that was before him.

The enemies of Nehemiah would not give up. They could not destroy Nehemiah, they could not distract him, and the they could not discourage him so they would try to deceive him. They would send false prophets and prophetesses to convince him to sin. One such prophet would try to convince him to seek refuge in the temple. Nehemiah was not a priest, and he knew that there would be great consequences for breaking God's law. Nehemiah was able to stand against the deception of his enemy because he knew the Word of God. Our enemy will seek to deceive us as well, and we must be armed with the Word of God to stand against his schemes and his deception. God's Word is our weapon and our defense. With God's Word in hand and God on our side, we can face every attack that the enemy can bring against us.

" GOD'S WORD IS OUR WEAPON
AND OUR DEFENSE

1 Our enemy seeks to destroy us, distract us, discourage us, and deceive us just as Nehemiah's enemies did. How does our enemy seek to do this?

2 What is the kingdom work that you have been called to do?

3 Nehemiah was able to be discerning and not deceived because he knew God's Word. Why is a knowledge of God's Word an essential weapon in the battle of the Christian life?

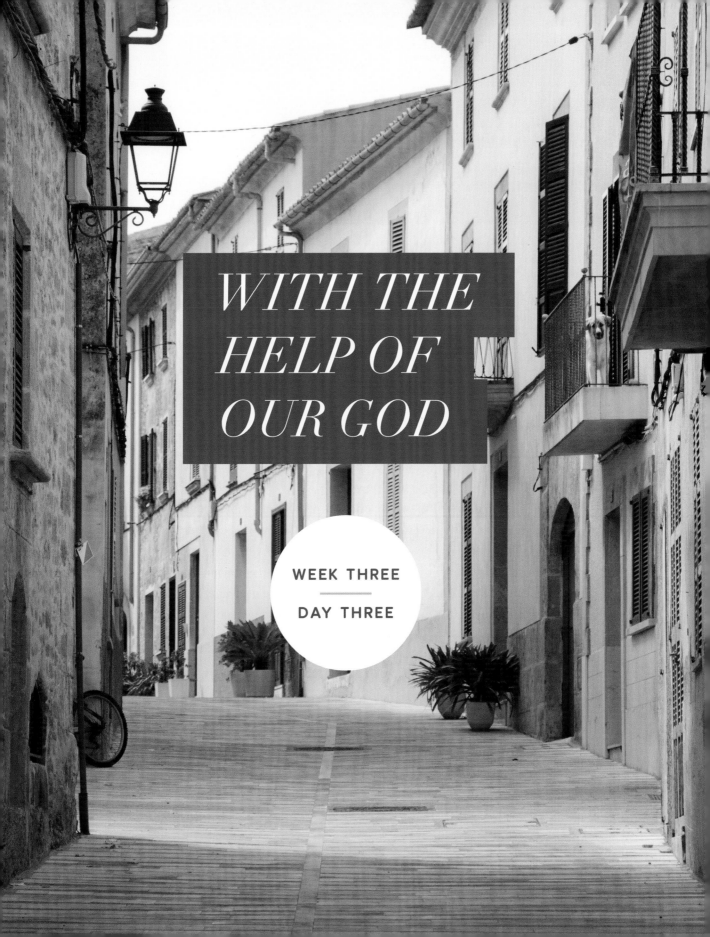

WITH THE HELP OF OUR GOD

WEEK THREE

DAY THREE

The work of building was complete, and yet in so many ways there was so much more to build. The book will now shift from the task of building the wall of Jerusalem to that of building up the people of God. Verse 15 opens with the matter of fact truth that they finished the wall. Despite every obstacle and ever opposition, the work was now completed. The wall was rebuilt in just fifty-two days. God's hand had been in the rebuilding of the wall from the beginning, and it is here in verse 16 that we see that not only did the people of God recognize that God's hand was in this, but even the enemies heard of the great work that had been done and knew that the God of Israel had helped His people. God used the rebuilding of the wall to show His power and faithfulness to His people and also to the surrounding nations. God's presence and power were evident in this work. May the presence and power of God be evident in our lives as well. In Nehemiah 4:14, Nehemiah had reminded the people to remember the Lord. There is no need to fear the enemy when we remember who God is. He will be faithful to His people.

Just because success had come in the building of the wall did not mean that the opposition disappeared. Tobiah was still around and taking up a new strategy. He had connections to Israel through both his business dealing and through marriage in his family, and he used his influence to try to sway the people away from Nehemiah's godly leadership. The attacks of Tobiah became personal toward Nehemiah, but Nehemiah would not be shaken. He knew that God had called him to a great task, and he would not abandon the work. The wall was now finished being rebuilt, but there was still work to be done in rebuilding the people of God. The rebuilding of the wall was not just about safety. It was ultimately about calling out God's people to be set apart and creating an environment for worship. The Westminster Shorter Catechism famously reminds us that the chief end of man is to glorify God and to enjoy Him forever. Even here in Nehemiah, this is what Nehemiah was working towards. He was seeking to build an environment where God's people could do what God had called them to do, where they could serve Him, sacrifice to Him, and worship Him.

Jerusalem was not just any other city. Jerusalem was the city of God and these were God's people. In chapter 7, we find a long list of names. It is a genealogy of the people of God. And though we may be tempted to skip past all of the names and numbers, they served a great purpose as Nehemiah reminded the people that they were God's people. They were people that had been called out of exile. They were the remnant that returned. They were God's servants serving in individual ways for the glory of God. As humans we are prone to forget. We forget the past. We forget how God has been faithful. We forget how He has answered prayer. And we forget who we are. Nehemiah did not want the people to forget. So he reminded them.

We are not too much different than the people in Nehemiah's day. We are prone to forget. We forget who we once were and how we were enslaved to sin. We forget that we have been rescued and redeemed. We forget that God has always been faithful. We need to preach the message of His faithfulness to ourselves over and over again. We need to remind ourselves of what He has done. We need to remind ourselves that we are His. In Nehemiah's day, the people and the enemy knew that God had been with them on this journey, and we can be assured of the same truth in our own life. If we are children of God, He is working in us and through us and victory is sure.

1 How has God's hand been seen in the book of Nehemiah?
Refer to Nehemiah 2:8, 2:12, 2:20, 4:15, and 4:20.

2 What are some of the obstacles that were encountered while building the wall? What obstacles have you encountered in your own life?

3 Why do we need to be reminded of who we are in Christ? How does our identity impact the way that we live our life?

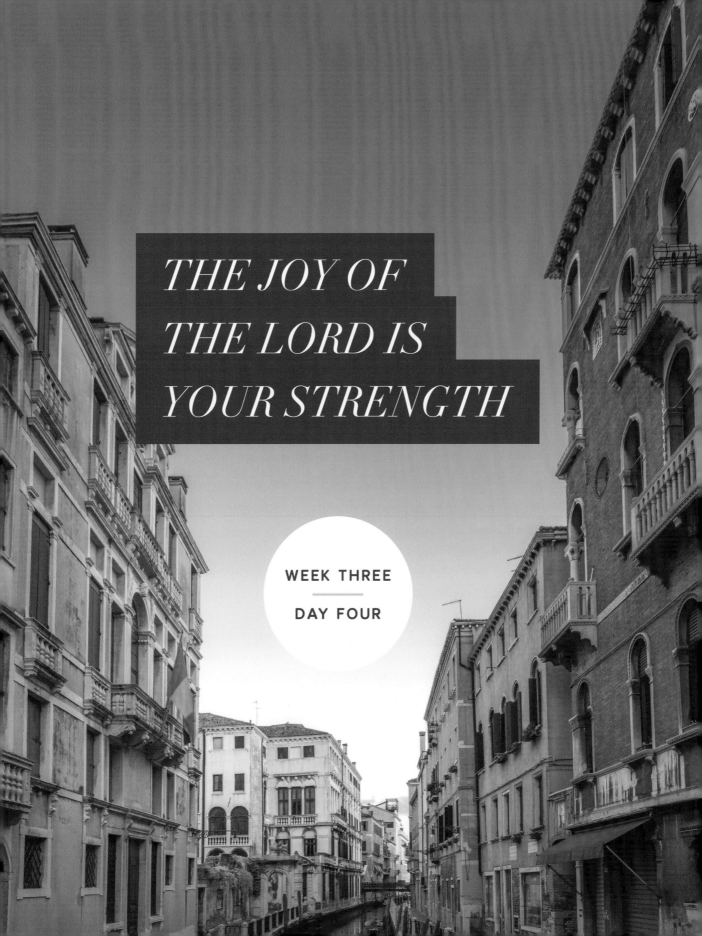

THE JOY OF THE LORD IS YOUR STRENGTH

WEEK THREE

DAY FOUR

NEHEMIAH 8:1-12

The wall was built, and now it was time to build up the people. The building of God's people is always rooted in the Word of God. It is God's Word that revives and restores the heart. The people wanted to hear the Word of God. Though you and I may have multiple copies of the Bible and free access to a multitude of translations online, the people in this time did not have a personal copy of God's Word. Many did not even speak Hebrew to be able to understand without interpretation and explanation. We see Ezra step onto the scene as the people ask him to read and explain God's Word. They read the Word of God for many hours. The text tells us that they read from early morning through midday. There is no grumbling about a sermon too long or restlessness among the people. The people were moved to worship. God's Word leaves us in awe of God. That is it's purpose. There is no revival without a renewed passion for God's Word. God's Word is a treasure to us, yet so often we neglect it for lesser pursuits. This passage points us back to our great need for Scripture.

We are not told that Ezra was an eloquent speaker or a gifted communicator. There is no mention of funny jokes or perfect sermon illustrations. We are simply told of the power of God's written Word. Faithful preaching and teaching need not be extravagant; it need only to be faithful to the text. This was teaching that interpreted and applied the words of Scripture. The Scripture was read, and the Scripture was explained. The reading and explaining of Scripture exalts Christ which should be the aim of all teaching, preaching, and Bible study. God is the subject of all of Scripture, so when we read and study His Word expositionally (book by book, verse by verse) we exalt Him, and we are compelled to worship as we stand in awe of the exalted One. We must never forget that God's presence is as near as opening His Word. When you don't know what to do, open His Word. When God feels far off, open His Word. When your heart is anxious, open His Word. When you need comfort, open His Word. His Word is what we need in every situation and in every circumstance.

The people began to weep in response to the reading of God's Word and the realization of their sin. Though there would soon be a time of repentance, Nehemiah reminded them that this was a time for celebration for all that God had done and for who He was. Nehemiah encouraged them to rejoice and said, "The joy of the LORD is your strength." Yahweh the covenant God had been faithful, and He would be faithful forevermore. The word translated as "strength" is also translated as "stronghold, refuge, or fortress." What an interesting reminder from Nehemiah immediately following the completion of the wall that was meant to be a physical refuge, strength, and fortress from the enemies. It is a reminder that though there was rejoicing over the physical wall that would protect them, it was the Lord Himself and the joy that He gives to His people that is the true refuge and strength of His children.

The joy of the Lord in the life of the child of God is a glimpse of restoration. God restores joy despite all that has been wounded and marked by sin and the fall. God redeems the most broken parts of our lives and replaces them with overflowing joy.

The section ends telling us that the people went away rejoicing because they had heard the Word of God and understood it. This should be our response to God's Word as well. Whether we are listening to our pastor preach or reading our Bible on our own. God's Word shows us who God is, and it points us to the good news of the gospel. It reminds us that God has a plan that He is working for our good. He has purpose for our past and our present, and He is already working a plan of faithfulness for our future. May we leave His Word rejoicing that the joy of the Lord is our strength.

1 Read the passage again and describe the scene. What do you think it would have been like to be there that day?

2 What was the response of the people to God's Word? What can we learn from how they responded?

3 Read Isaiah 12, Psalm 27:1, Psalm 28:8, and Psalm 31:2. What do you think it means that the joy of the Lord is our strength?

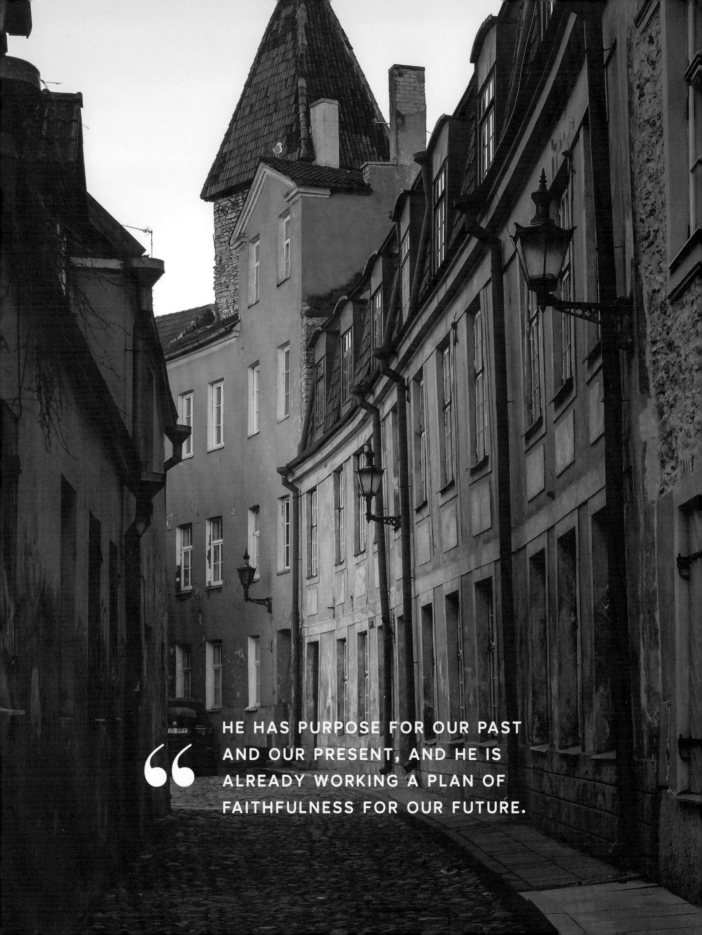

HE HAS PURPOSE FOR OUR PAST
AND OUR PRESENT, AND HE IS
ALREADY WORKING A PLAN OF
FAITHFULNESS FOR OUR FUTURE.

REMEMBERING THE GOODNESS OF GOD

WEEK THREE

DAY FIVE

NEHEMIAH 8:13-18

God's people had just opened God's Word and stood in awe of the beauty it contained. We now come to the very next day, and we see another gathering of the men. It seems the women had likely taken the children back home, and now the men gathered to open God's Word again. But something amazing happened as they opened the Scriptures. The people were made aware of what needed to be done and were compelled to obedience by the record of God's Word. God's Word urges us to action. God's Word reveals to us what we should do, and then God, through His Spirit in us, gives us the power to do it. Our obedience is an evidence of our love for God (1 John 5:2).

As they read God's Word, they were reminded of the Feast of Booths, or Feast Tabernacles, that needed to be observed. They could have made a resolution or planned to do that next year, but instead they immediately obeyed. They didn't worry about the fact that things were not prepared, they simply got to work. The feasts were something that God had instituted to commemorate what He had done for His people. The feasts each celebrated a specific aspect of God's faithfulness. The Feast of Booths celebrated the fact that God had provided for and protected the people while they wandered in the wilderness after the exodus had them living in tents. It celebrated how God protected His people in difficult circumstances and how He provided manna for them in the wilderness each day. Though we do not celebrate these Old Testament feasts, we would be wise to celebrate God's faithfulness as well. These feasts facilitated a time set aside for remembering God's faithfulness. We are prone to wander and need to be reminded as well of God's faithfulness. We need to keep the character of God in front of us constantly. This is why we celebrate the Lord's Supper, and this is why we gather each week with the church to celebrate the resurrection. There is great value in the spiritual disciplines, whether meeting with the body of Christ or opening His Word in our personal time. These sacred habits consistently point us back to God despite how the world tries to distract us from Him. We need to *remember*.

At the center of this celebration and remembrance was the Word of God. The Word of God should be the central focus of our gatherings as well. The time of year that the Feast of Booths took place is significant. It took place right before the harvest, and the people would ask God to bless them with rain. They were asking God to provide rain for them just as He had provided water from a rock for Moses so many years before. After the reminder of His faithfulness so many years ago, they would ask Him to be faithful to them now. Though this wasn't part of the initial feast, it is spoken of several times throughout Scripture. We see references to it in Zechariah 14:16-19 and Isaiah 12:2-6. In fact, as we come to the New Testament, we see Jesus Himself participating in the Feast of Booths. We see the account of what happened during the Feast of Booths in John 7, and in John 7:37-38 at the end of the Feast we see Jesus make a bold and beautiful claim to be the living water specifically when read in the context of the Feast of Booths. The people were looking for water, and Jesus was telling them that He was what they were really longing for.

The Feast of Booths pointed to Jesus. It was a glimpse of hope. It was a reminder that the same God who had brought protection and provision in the wilderness would bring the Messiah who would be the greatest protector and provider the people could ever ask for. Moses had delivered the people through the wilderness, but Jesus would deliver their souls. And because of Jesus who is the living water, every thirsty heart could be satisfied. We can run to Jesus as well. He is the source of our provision and protection, and Jesus is the water that quenches the thirst of our hearts.

1 The Feasts were meant to cause the people to remember God and what He had done for them. Write down some things that you need to remember that God has done for you.

2 Hebrew tradition tells us that rabbis claimed you had not known true happiness unless you had been in Jerusalem for the Feast of Booths. Nehemiah had reminded the people to find their joy and strength in the Lord. Read Isaiah 12:2–6. How does remembering God's faithfulness bring us joy?

3 Read John 7:37–38. In what ways is Jesus like water for our thirsty souls?

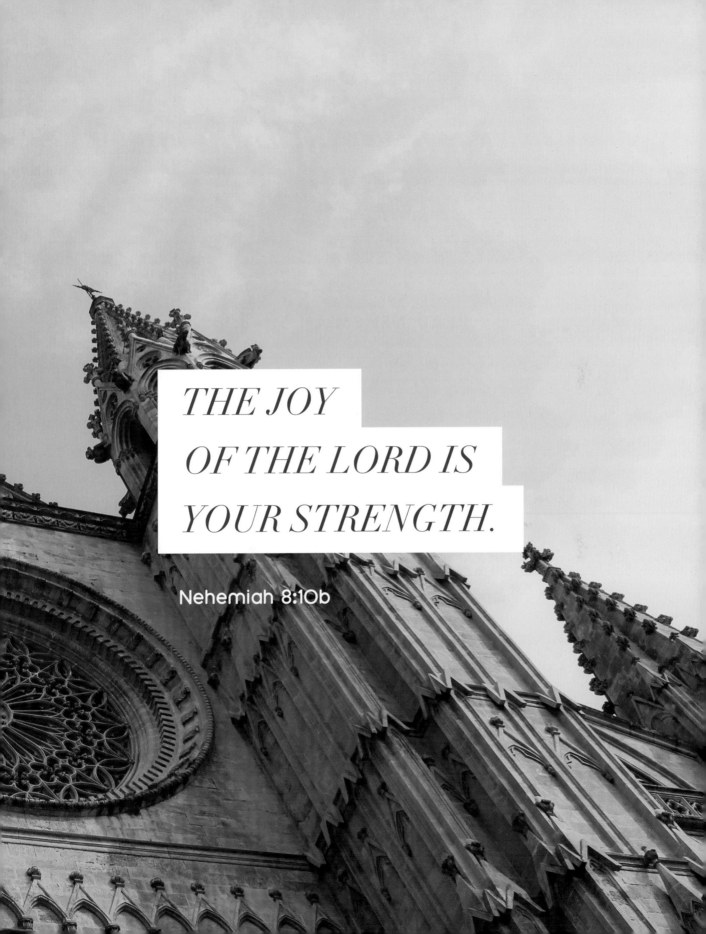

THE JOY OF THE LORD IS YOUR STRENGTH.

Nehemiah 8:10b

WEEK THREE REFLECTION

READ NEHEMIAH 5:1–8:18

Paraphrase the passage from this week.

What did you observe from this week's text about God and His character?

What does the passage teach about the condition of mankind and about yourself?

How does this passage point to the gospel?

How should you respond to this passage? What is the personal application?

What specific action steps can you take this week to apply the passage?

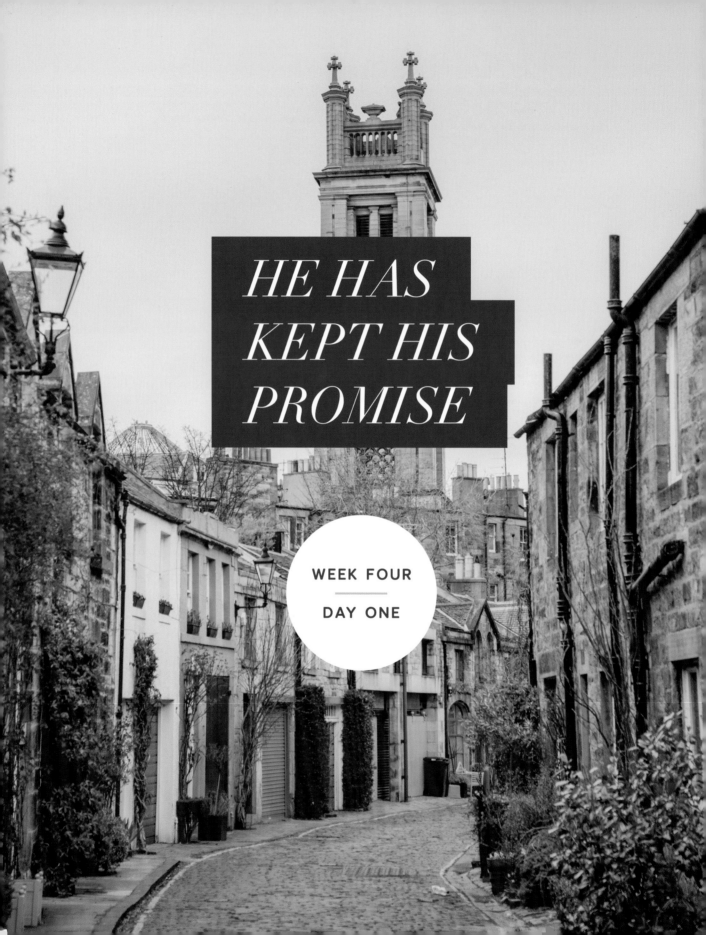

HE HAS KEPT HIS PROMISE

WEEK FOUR

—

DAY ONE

NEHEMIAH 9:1-8

The Feast of Booths has now ended, but the people will come together again to worship the Lord. In chapter 8, the people had been broken by their sin and compelled to mourn and weep over their sin. Nehemiah had told them during that time that it wasn't a time to mourn, but a time to rejoice because the joy of the Lord was their strength. It had been almost a month that had been dedicated to worship and celebrating all that God had done, but now the time had come for the people to mourn the sin that was heavy on their hearts. There are times and seasons for rejoicing and there are times and seasons for mourning and weeping over our sin (Ecclesiastes 3:1-8). The time had come to mourn, but they would not mourn without hope.

Confession is not usually on our list of favorite things to do, but confession restores our hearts to the Lord. When we confess sin, we get rid of the things that stand between us and God (Isaiah 59:2). Confession restores fellowship. David spoke of the importance of brokenness in Psalm 51, and Jesus spoke of how we should mourn for our sin in the Sermon on the Mount in Matthew 5:4. However, we often want fellowship with God without the confession of our sin. But we have a promise that when we confess, He will forgive (1 John 1:9). Forgiveness brings freedom, and forgiveness heals the brokenness of our hearts.

The people then pour their hearts out in prayer to the Lord. This prayer is one of the longest prayers of Scripture, and it is also one of the most detailed and condensed summaries of the Old Testament. The people are recounting the faithfulness of God by recounting their history. The Levites called to the people to arise and bless the Lord. The worshipful prayer flowed out of hearts that were seeking to renew the covenant. They were desperately aware of their sin, and they were also overwhelmed by grace. They began at creation. This is likely because they had been reading the Torah for the past month, so they started at the beginning. They declared that God alone had made the world (Deuteronomy 6:4). God created the world with the power of His Word, and all of creation worships the Creator.

Then they moved to Abraham and the Abrahamic covenant that God made with Abraham. God had called Abraham (referred to as Abram at the time) out of his home in Ur. He called him to be set apart, and He promised to him a land, a people, and a worldwide blessing that would come through him. Abraham was just a man. He struggled to trust and even tried to do things in his own way, but God was faithful to him. When Abraham died, he and his wife Sarah had just one son named Isaac. It didn't seem like the start of a great nation, but God was working. Verse 8 tells us that God found Abraham faithful. The faithfulness of Abraham is not a testament to his own good works or to anything about himself. Abraham is not a superhero; he was just a man. He was a simple man that placed his faith in an extraordinary God. God had chosen him and called him out, and Abraham by faith simply followed God into the unknown. He trusted when things didn't make sense, and God rewarded him for his obedience that was driven by simple faith.

The end of verse 8 makes clear what happened with that covenant that God made to Abraham. God had kept, or fulfilled, what He had promised to do because of who He is. The people in the time of Nehemiah couldn't even see the full extent of God's faithfulness. That would be seen only in Jesus, but they could see enough to know that God was faithful. It is interesting to note that the word here that is translated as "kept" or "fulfilled" is the same Hebrew word that has been translated throughout the book as "arise." Throughout the book, the people have been called to arise. They have been compelled to arise and build a wall. Nehemiah has arisen to pray. And they have been commanded to arise and bless the Lord, and here we see that God also arises. God arises to be faithful to His people. God arises to keep His promises and fulfill His covenants.

We have much to learn in these short verses. We are called to confession and worship. We are called to remember His faithfulness. We are called to be holy and set apart for the Lord. And we are called to arise and to watch Him arise and be faithful to all that He has said He will do.

1 Why do we resist confession? Why is confession important?
Psalm 51 and 1 John 1:9 can give you insight.

2 Read Deuteronomy 6:4. Nehemiah 9:6 is a restatement of this verse that
was one of the most important parts of God's Word to the people of Israel
that were surrounded by nations who worshiped many false gods. How is
the reminder that it is God alone that is the Lord important for us today?

3 This first section of the prayer ends with a reminder that God has arisen
and kept His promise because of who He is. How does this give you insight
into God's working in your own life?

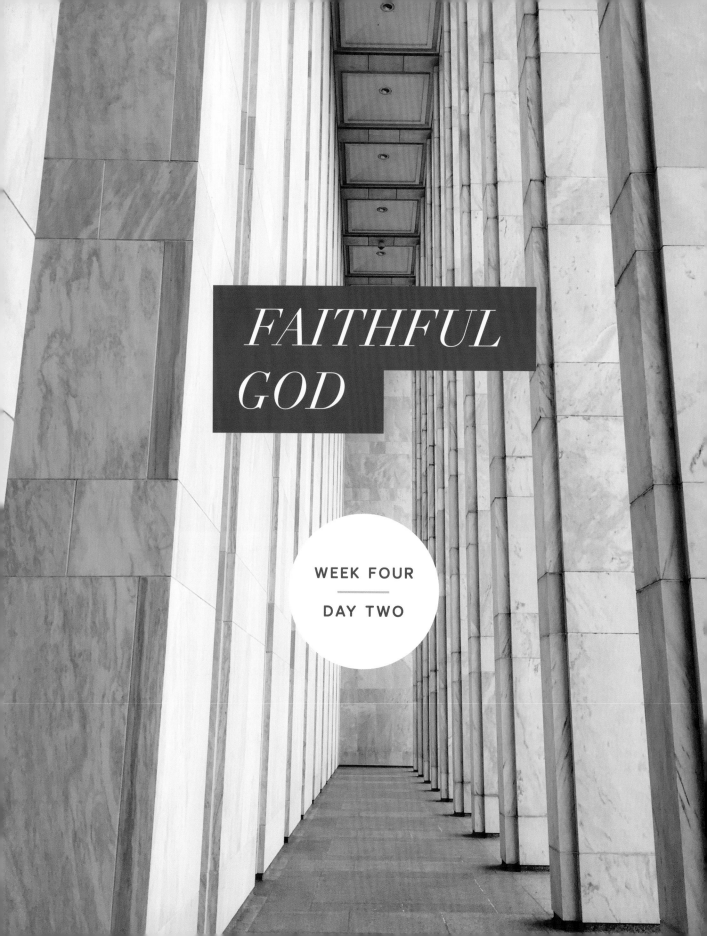

FAITHFUL GOD

WEEK FOUR

DAY TWO

NEHEMIAH 9:9-21

This section of this beautiful prayer takes us back to Exodus. We have a front row view to how God worked and how His people responded to His covenant faithfulness. In the first section of the prayer we saw the creation and God's covenant with Abraham. Now we see one of the ways that God kept that covenant by delivering His people from Egypt. As we look back, we cannot help but see the symbolism of our own redemption in the redemption story of Israel from Egypt. The same God that delivered Israel from the bondage of Egypt has delivered us from the bondage of sin.

Reading through this passage, we cannot help but be overwhelmed by a God that works on behalf of His people. Verse after verse tells of all that God did to rescue and redeem His chosen people. This prayer is a model for us in so many ways. One of the things that we observe from reading this prayer is our great need to be God-focused. The prayer is centered on who God is and what He has done for His people. This section is the perfect example of that. The beginning of the passage reads almost like a list of all the things that God has done. It is a reminder of who He is and how He works on behalf of His people. From God seeing the affliction of His people to delivering them as they walked through the Red Sea on dry land, to providing for them in the wilderness, God was with them every step of the way.

Yet in verse 21 we come to a very important word. *But.* Despite all that God had done for the people of Israel. Despite the miracles that He had worked for them and the ways that He had delivered them and cared for them, they chose to rebel against Him. The people that He had delivered refused to obey and were not mindful of all that He had done for them. They ignored His commands and His ways, and they ignored Him. The people were so set on disobedience that they appointed a leader to return them to Egypt. What!?! Back to slavery? It doesn't make sense. It is ridiculous. But sadly, this is how sin works. It doesn't make sense, but it tricks us into thinking that it is easier than following God into the unknown. Sin is easier than surrender. It is easier, but it is not better. Sin leads to death and brokenness. Surrender leads to life and joy. This passage shows us the seriousness of the sin of the people of Israel but also of our own sin. Sin is not something we should mess with; it is something we should run from. In verse 16, we saw how the word "but" shifted the entire passage, and in verse 17 it does it again. Despite the people that were arrogant and rebellious, we are given a description of God that should cause us to mourn our own sin and rejoice in our salvation. Despite the rebellion of the people and the fact that they were prone to wander, God was ever faithful. We are told that God is ready to forgive, full of grace and mercy, slow to anger, and overflowing with faithful and steadfast hesed love. The love that pursues and never fails. It is the never giving up kind of love. Verse 18 reinforces the truth for us by telling us that even when the people worshiped an idol, God did not forsake them. He is a merciful and faithful God. Instead of rejecting them, God ran to them. He guided them through the wilderness with a pillar of cloud and a pillar of fire. He guided with His Spirit, and He gave them everything that they needed. He sustained them, and verse 21 tells us that they lacked nothing.

How easy it is for us to roll our eyes at the stubborn Israelites when our hearts are just like theirs. We would so often rather be in bondage to our sin because it is where we are comfortable. We would rather complain than trust. We would rather worship idols of our own imagination than the true and living God that has delivered us. We would rather head back to Egypt than walk into the promised land. We feel like maybe we have been forgotten by God, or that perhaps others have gotten the better end of the deal. But we lack nothing when we have Him. He pursues us, and He is faithful. So we are going to have to allow truth to take charge of our feelings. We are going to have to live with hearts centered on the gospel and not just our feelings because our feelings are lying to us! We have Jesus. We lack nothing.

" WE LACK NOTHING
WHEN WE HAVE HIM.

1 Read through the passage again and write down or mark every action that God did. What does this tell you about how God works for His people?

2 Paraphrase this portion of the prayer. Think through how it could be spoken of your own life. What has God done for you? How have you responded?

3 Write down what this passage says about who God is. How does this impact the way that you trust God to work in your own situation?

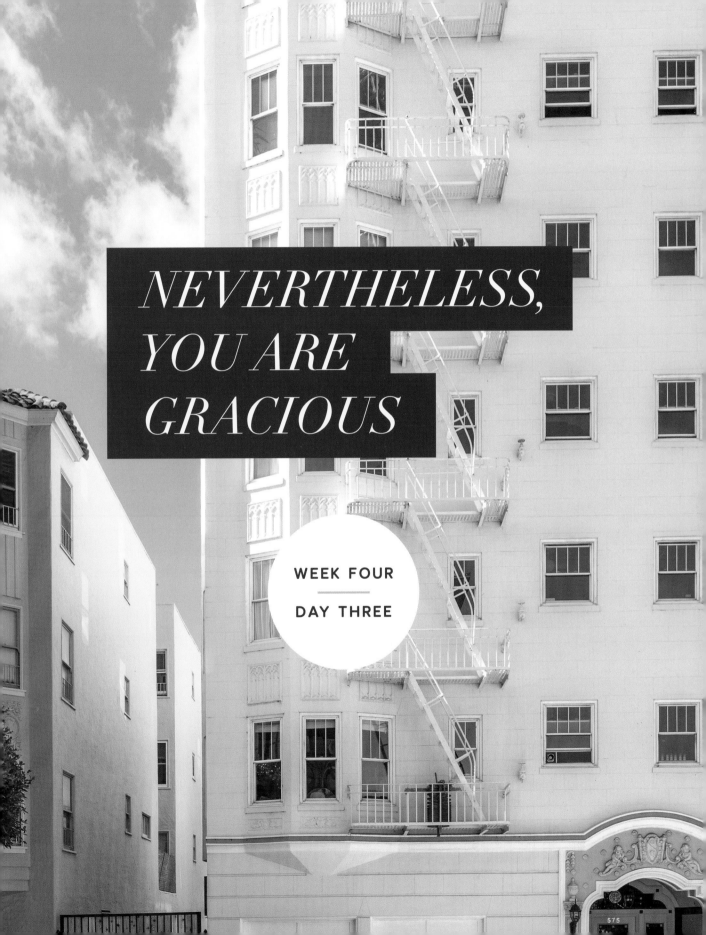

NEVERTHELESS, YOU ARE GRACIOUS

WEEK FOUR

DAY THREE

NEHEMIAH 9:22-31

This prayer contained in the book of Nehemiah is a stunning overview of the Old Testament and a beautiful picture of who God is and how He deals with His people. This beautiful prayer has covered the first five books of Scripture for us, and now the prayer picks up with the events of the book of Joshua and goes all the way through the prophets. After God had provided for them everything that they needed through the wilderness, He brought them into the promised land. God kept the promises that He had made to Abraham, including the promise that his children would be multiplied like the stars of heaven (Genesis 15). God gave the people victory over their enemies. God gave them everything they could have ever desired, but He longed for them to desire Him.

The people took the good gifts of God, but they rejected the Giver. They wanted all that God had to offer, but they did not want Him. They thought they knew so much better than the Lord, and they rebelled again. They rejected the law of God, and even killed the prophets that God had sent to warn them of their sin. The period of the judges is covered in verses 27-28, and we see how Israel rejected God in a cycle of disobedience through that time. Yet God in His faithfulness raised up judges to deliver them from the mess that they had made. The section ends by telling of the many years that God was patient or "bore with them" by sending them prophets to warn them and call them to repentance. But the people would not listen. Time after time they would reject God and insult His gracious favor towards them.

Throughout this section we are reminded of who God is. We see Him as a tender and loving Redeemer who is constantly pursuing His people who have chosen to rebel against Him. In Nehemiah 9:19, 26, 27, 28, and 31, we see a word in the Hebrew that is usually translated as "mercy" or "compassion." It is the Hebrew word *racham*. The direct translation of this word is "womb," and it points us to the way that our God loved Israel and the way that He loves us as well. Like a mother loves the unborn child she carries in her body with tender and merciful compassion, so our God loves us. He is willing to do anything for us. The response of Israel was time and time again to rebel, to refuse to listen, to forget, and to serve idols. Yet in tender and loving mercy and compassion, God in His longsuffering fought for Israel, pursued Israel, and showed them mercy. The section ends with a reminder that He is a gracious and merciful God.

We are not unlike Israel. We forget what God has done for us. We chase after idols. We seek after His gifts without running to the Giver. Yet just as He did in all of the Old Testament, God stands in grace and mercy calling us back to Himself. And every time we return, He stands with arms wide open and ready to receive us. So often we are like Israel. We reject the Lord, and we choose our own path. We often reject His plan to follow paths that simply lead to heartbreak, and yet He is waiting for us. He is tenderly calling us to stop trying to live this life in our own strength and choose to trust Him. He pleads with us to *surrender*.

So we have a choice. Will we choose our own path and do our own thing, or will we surrender and trust the One who knows the end from the beginning, the One who is working for the good of His people? Will we allow our hearts to return to the God who is ever gracious and merciful and always pursuing our hearts?

" GOD STANDS IN GRACE
AND MERCY CALLING US
BACK TO HIMSELF

1 Read through the passage again. Mark all of the transition words such as therefore, but, and, so, yet, nevertheless, etc. What do you observe from these words?

2 Read through the passage and mark all of the actions done by the nation of Israel and all of the actions done by God. What stands out to you?

3 What does this tell you about who God is and how He deals with His children?

RENEWING THE COVENANT

WEEK FOUR

DAY FOUR

NEHEMIAH 9:32-38

The Levites have spent the entire chapter up until this point recounting the sin of the nation of Israel and the faithfulness and grace of God. Time and time again, Israel had rebelled against the Lord, and God had extended mercy to them. As we come to this final section of Nehemiah 9, we will see the Levites plead on behalf of the people and then be willing to step into action. The people were compelled to repentance due to a glimpse of who God is. When we glimpse the glory of God, everything changes. When we see who He is and we begin to grasp how He perfectly embodies love and holiness, mercy and justice, righteousness and grace, we will stand in awe of Him. *The glory of God shifts our perspective.*

So verse 32 begins with the Levites describing the Lord. Though He is too majestic and glorious to describe, they try their best to put into words who He is as they have been doing for the entire chapter. He is great and so much more important than anything else in this world. He is mighty. He is the warrior of His people who fights our battles and conquers our foes. He is the awesome God, and we stand in awe of who He is. He is the God who keeps covenant. Though Israel had failed over and over again, He never went back on His Word. He keeps steadfast love. He never gives up or turns His back on His people. This is His *hesed* love that pursues us and seeks us out. They appeal to God not on the basis of their own righteousness (they had none), but on the basis of who He is. They have laid out before Him the story of the people of Israel. The nation had been faithless and rebellious. They had been complainers, and they had run after idols. But God in His steadfast love and mercy pursued them and loved them.

The people knew that the situation that they were in was of their own doing and that they deserved the discipline of the Lord. Everything that God had done was righteous (Nehemiah 9:33). God had been faithful to them, and they had rejected Him. He had pursued them, and they had done all they could to try to hide from Him. But you cannot hide from God. He saw their rebellion and sin—and He loved them anyway. He loved them not because of any good they had done, but because He had chosen them and set His love on them.

The people were moved to repentance as they looked at their own sin and saw God's goodness. They are asking God to do it again. He had been faithful and merciful and gracious, and now they plead, "Lord, do it again." They are asking Him to be who He is. They are asking Him to display His character. This was not just an empty promise from the people. The Levites are prepared for action. They want to renew the covenant, and they want to do it in writing. They set this moment as a memorial and a reminder to them of the promise that they had made to God. May we have this same desire. May we yearn to turn from our sin and run to our Savior. May we repent and confess. May we abandon our love of the world for a love of His Word.

But this passage points us to something even greater than revival and covenant renewal. You see, the people renewing this covenant where just that—people. The gospel reminds us that we are fallen, and our fallen state means that no matter how hard we try, we can never live up to God's standard. So they would try and they would write the covenant that we will study in chapter 10, but ultimately they would fail, because that is what humans do. But this moment points to a need that burned inside them on that day. The need for the Messiah. Jesus is the answer to their failures and to ours. Because Jesus is the One that would bring a new covenant, a covenant better than any covenant before (Jeremiah 31:31-34, Ezekiel 37:26-28, Luke 22:20, Hebrews 8). This covenant wouldn't be about reformed actions, but about transformed hearts. The answer to our weakness, and our sin, and our unfaithfulness, and our lack of trust is not in ourselves. *It is Jesus.*

1 The people were compelled to repentance when they saw who God is. How does the glory of God shift our perspective?

2 How does this passage give insight into the love that God has for His people?

3 Jesus is the mediator of the new covenant. This new and better covenant would not just seek to change the actions of the people, but to change their hearts. Read Jeremiah 31:31–34, Ezekiel 37:26–28, Luke 22:20, and Hebrews 8 and write down any observations about the new covenant and how it was different than the Old Testament system of sacrifices and following the law.

ALL IN

WEEK FOUR

DAY FIVE

NEHEMIAH 10

With hearts that were broken over their sin and stirred to serve God, the people would sign their names to a covenant. We see a list of names and groups of people that put their name on the list. Nehemiah as a true and godly leader is the first to sign. Signing the covenant was their way of saying "I am all in." Priests and leaders added their names, foreigners that had been converted added their names, one by one the people had a choice to make. They had to choose if they were on God's side and if they would be faithful to do what He had commanded them to do in light of the grace that He had shown them. This was a commitment to follow God's Word (Nehemiah 10:29). It was a commitment to live God's way. As we read these words we can almost hear the call to our own hearts; *"Are you all in?" "Are you ready to sign your name?"* Salvation should lead to surrender. We can trust our God to be faithful, and this compels us to trust that His way is best.

It is not explicitly mentioned in the book of Nehemiah, but in the process of the celebrating of God's goodness, reading the law, and keeping the feasts would have been the celebration of the Day of Atonement. It was on this day that a scapegoat was brought forth. This scapegoat would be a representation of what Jesus has done for us. The sins of the people would be confessed over that goat and then the goat would be set free into the wilderness never to be seen again. Just as Jesus carries our sin away to be seen no more, so the goat would run carrying the weight of the people's sin. It is after this time of confession and repentance that commitment is made to follow in the ways of God. Derek W. H. Thomas says, "It is meant to illustrate the "gospel grammar" of Scripture, Old Testament as much as New: the imperative follows the indicative; the promise of obedience is made in the wake of the experience of grace; their obedience was an indication of thankful hearts for forgivingness that had already been given." The people were not trying to earn God's favor by doing all the right things; He had already showered them in mercy and grace. Now they responded out of grateful obedience. This wasn't about legalism. They were not adding extra rules or trying to earn God's favor; they were living in light of God's favor. *Hearts touched by grace yearn to obey.*

The covenant would specifically mention a few key areas, though it was a commitment to follow all of the Torah. The first topic brought up was that of intermarriage. The people would commit not to marry those outside of Israel. This can be hard for us in our culture to understand, but this commandment had nothing to do with race and everything to do with a relationship with God. Just as believers in the New Testament are commanded to not be unequally yoked with unbelievers (2 Corinthians 6:14), the people of the Old Testament were commanded not to marry those that worshiped idols and false gods. Marriage is at its core a picture of God's relationship to His people. It is a one-flesh union that should be a beautiful picture of the unity of the believer to God, but this picture is tainted if one spouse is not a believer and this unity is broken. Though many find themselves in a marriage that is not unified, and Scripture even speaks to this situation (1 Peter 3:1), it is not something that should be pursued. The other areas covered in this covenant agreement were keeping the Sabbath and sabbatical year and supporting the temple. Both of these were an act of trust in the Lord for provision. The people had to trust that God would faithfully provide for their needs while they obeyed what had been commanded to them. The question is posed to us as well. *Will we obey when God's plan doesn't make sense? Will we trust Him even then?* Each one of these areas was pointing to God. Our love for God should impact every area of our lives. There should be nothing that is not measured by God's Word. There is no sacred and secular. Every moment of our life is part of the sacred, because every moment is an opportunity to trust God and choose His way and not our own.

1 Read through the beginning of the chapter and record the different groups of people that committed to the covenant. In what ways can we make a commitment to follow God?

2 The heart of the covenant was for the people to obey God's Word. In what ways can you obey God's Word in your own life?

3 What does this passage tell us about how God values obedience from a heart of worship? How do the previous chapters we have studied help your understanding of what is happening in chapter 10?

YOU, LORD, ARE THE ONLY GOD. YOU CREATED THE HEAVENS, THE HIGHEST HEAVENS WITH ALL THEIR STARS, THE EARTH AND ALL THAT IS ON IT, THE SEAS AND ALL THAT IS IN THEM. YOU GIVE LIFE TO ALL OF THEM, AND ALL THE STARS OF HEAVEN WORSHIP YOU.

Nehemiah 9:6

WEEK FOUR REFLECTION

READ NEHEMIAH 9:1–10:39

Paraphrase the passage from this week.

What did you observe from this week's text about God and His character?

What does the passage teach about the condition of mankind and about yourself?

How does this passage point to the gospel?

How should you respond to this passage? What is the personal application?

What specific action steps can you take this week to apply the passage?

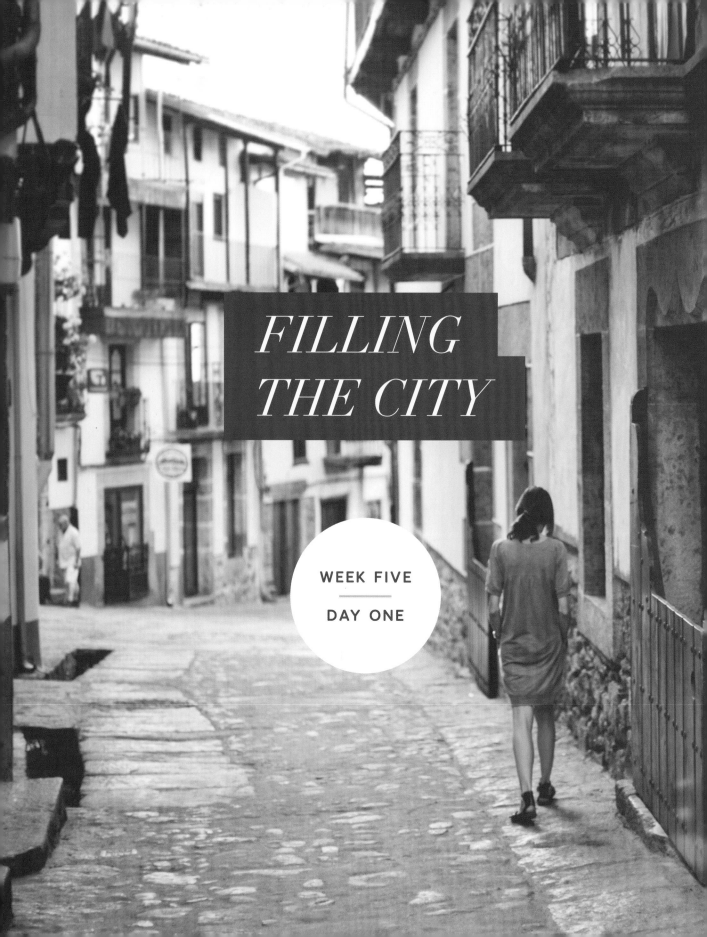

FILLING THE CITY

WEEK FIVE

—

DAY ONE

NEHEMIAH 11:1-12:26

In chapters 11 and 12, we see the task of repopulating the city taking place. The wall had been completed and the temple was ready, but now people needed to move back into Jerusalem. Things were not perfect in Jerusalem and there was still much work to be done, but God had called His people to arise and rebuild and now it was time for some of the people to move into town. The book of Nehemiah takes place in a time when land ownership was especially important for the financial success of a family. It was from crops and animals that a family would find its income. So moving into the city would be a sacrifice for many. But it was one that was worth it. Some people were chosen and others would voluntarily choose to go and submit their lives to the service of God in Jerusalem. The occupations mentioned in the chapter center on the temple worship that was reinstituted. In order for this vital part of Jerusalem to run smoothly, there would need to be musicians, and scribes, and gatekeepers, and all kinds of temple workers. There were a variety of people and a variety of gifts. This is how life in the kingdom works. God gifts us each individually to be able to accomplish kingdom work.

Verse 2 tells us that the people blessed all those that willingly went to do the work in Jerusalem and gave their lives to kingdom work. Serving God often involves sacrifice and laying aside our own plans to do what God has called us to do. The people that went willingly are a demonstration for us of what it means to serve God and to humbly follow wherever He leads. But they also point us to Jesus Himself who humbled Himself and became a man. He was born as a helpless baby and placed in a lowly manger in Bethlehem. He lived a perfect life. He healed the sick and gave sight to the blind while being ridiculed by religious leaders. He died on a cross and willingly laid down His life for our salvation. Jesus emptied Himself so that we could be filled with eternal life (Philippians 2:5-11). The Christian life is a life of surrender. It is a life of looking to Jesus and allowing Him to transform us into His image from the inside out.

The things that seemed so far off in chapters 1 and 2 were now coming about. God had been faithful and He had done what He had said He would do. The walls had been rebuilt and the hearts of the people had been rebuilt as well. God had called the people to arise and build, and God had arisen and been faithful to them every step of the way. In Nehemiah 1:9, Nehemiah had prayed the words of Moses and the promise of God that God would dwell with His people—and that is exactly what had taken place. The worship of the temple was restored and God's people had been restored by the power of God's Word. And with the power of God's Word working in their hearts, the people were ready and willing to serve God and to build the city of God.

These lists of names are not always our favorites. We have mentioned that before. They can feel long and tedious and we don't always understand the point of it all. But for the people of Nehemiah's day, these were their names. This was a declaration that God had been faithful to them and that now they would show their gratitude with faithful service to Him. This is a list of the faithful and valiant servants of God who choose His kingdom and glory above their own. If a list was made today of those that are faithful, would your name be on the list? Would you be named with the faithful servants of God? Would you be one that goes willingly with the spirit of Christ? By God's grace may we be faithful to the cause of the gospel.

1 Read Nehemiah 11:6, 8, and 14 again. In each of these verses, most translations include the phrase "valiant men," or "men of valor." Look up the word "valiant" in the dictionary. Record the meaning of the word and how we can be people of valor as we seek to serve God.

2 Read Philippians 2:5–11. What does this tell us about the character and humility of God? How can we display this same spirit in our own lives?

3 How may God be asking you to willingly serve Him? How can you encourage and bless others that willingly serve God with their lives?

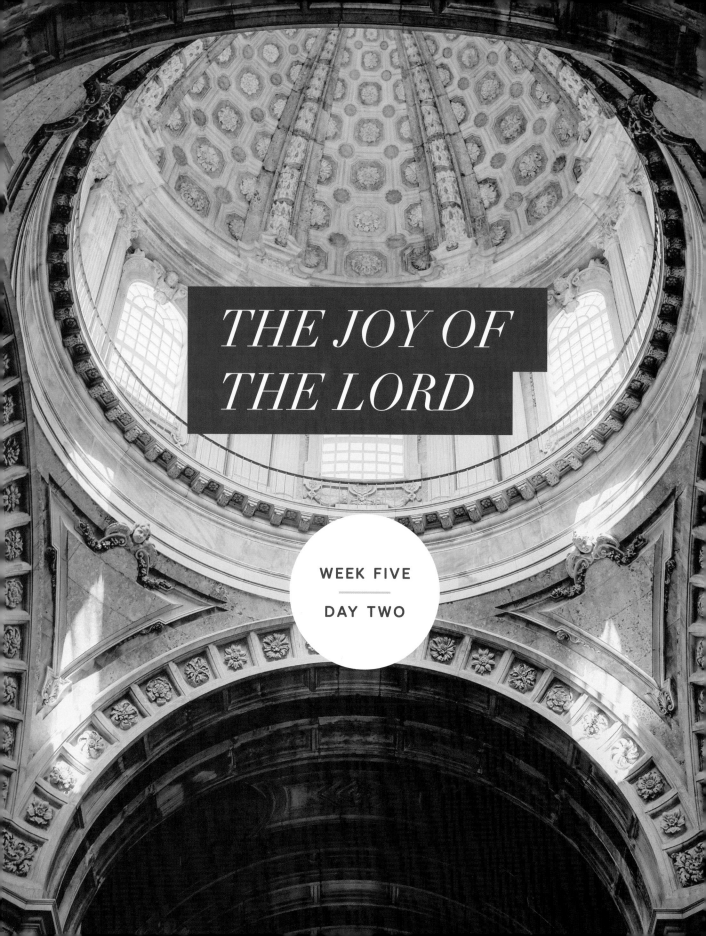

THE JOY OF THE LORD

WEEK FIVE

DAY TWO

NEHEMIAH 12:27-47

It was time for the wall to be dedicated to the Lord. The people had labored, and now they were dedicating their work and their city to God. This section begins with the Levites being called from their homes to come for the celebration. The Levites would serve for two weeks out of the year and the rest of the year they would be in their homes, but this celebration was a cause for all of the Levites to come to the holy city (1 Chronicles 24). God's people would gather together in Jerusalem for this celebration and dedication.

Before the dedication could take place, the priests and Levites as well as the people would need to be purified. This ritual of purification was a symbol that the people were being set apart as God's holy people. It was a symbol of the need for spiritual cleansing. As God's people today, we are made pure by Jesus' blood. Jesus took on sin for us so that we would be made the righteousness of God (2 Corinthians 5:21). Now, if we are in Christ, when God looks at us, He sees the righteousness of His Son. We are made pure because of the blood of the Pure One.

The people were filled with joy as they came to this dedication. The work was finished. The people were revived by the power of God's Word. And God had been faithful. Choirs of worshipers sang on top of the wall that had been in ruin just weeks before. The people stood on the wall that the enemy had said would never hold up a fox (Nehemiah 4:2-3). Can you imagine the joy that filled their hearts as they looked around at all that God had done. They sang in worship because God had been faithful.

This section of Scripture is in many ways the climax of the second half of the book. God had helped them rebuild the wall, and then He had rebuilt His people. He had centered their hearts on His Word and He had reminded them of the covenant. The theme of this section of Scripture is joy. The people were overwhelmed with joy as they dedicated the temple that day. Joy is cultivated in our hearts when we see who God is and recognize His faithfulness. As Christians, we should be people of joy and people of song, but this joy doesn't happen accidentally. It happens when we open God's Word and learn who He is. It happens when we purposefully recognize what God has done. It happens when we take time to see God's providential hand in every area of our lives. The people could have looked at the wall and thought about how great they were for accomplishing this work, but they knew that they were not the ones that had done it. God had done it, and they were joyful that He had chosen to use them in this great work. We must be careful to look at our own lives and recognize that everything that we have is a demonstration of God's faithful hand in our lives. Everything we have is because of who He is. Every breath we take is because of His matchless grace. Every moment is a gift of His grace to us, even the ones we do not understand.

As the passage ends, we see that the people structure their life around the Lord. They followed the law and wanted to worship the Lord. As the people of God, we seek to serve the Lord out of an overflow of joy and gratitude for what He has done for us. He has been abundantly faithful, and now our hearts' desire is to be His faithful servants.

The people saw the old, broken-down wall made new and they rejoiced. We look back at our past, our brokenness, and our sin, and see that Jesus has made us new. The people rejoiced at a new wall—we rejoice that we are a new creation (2 Corinthians 5:17). We have something to praise about. The gospel is our reason for joy.

" JOY IS CULTIVATED IN OUR HEARTS WHEN WE SEE WHO GOD IS AND RECOGNIZE HIS FAITHFULNESS.

1 Take a moment to picture the scene on this dedication day and describe it below. What do you think it would have been like to be there that day?

2 Read Psalm 48, 122, and 126. These are some of the psalms believed to have been sung on this day. How do these psalms lead you to praise in your own life?

3 Joy must be cultivated. How can you actively cultivate joy in your own life?

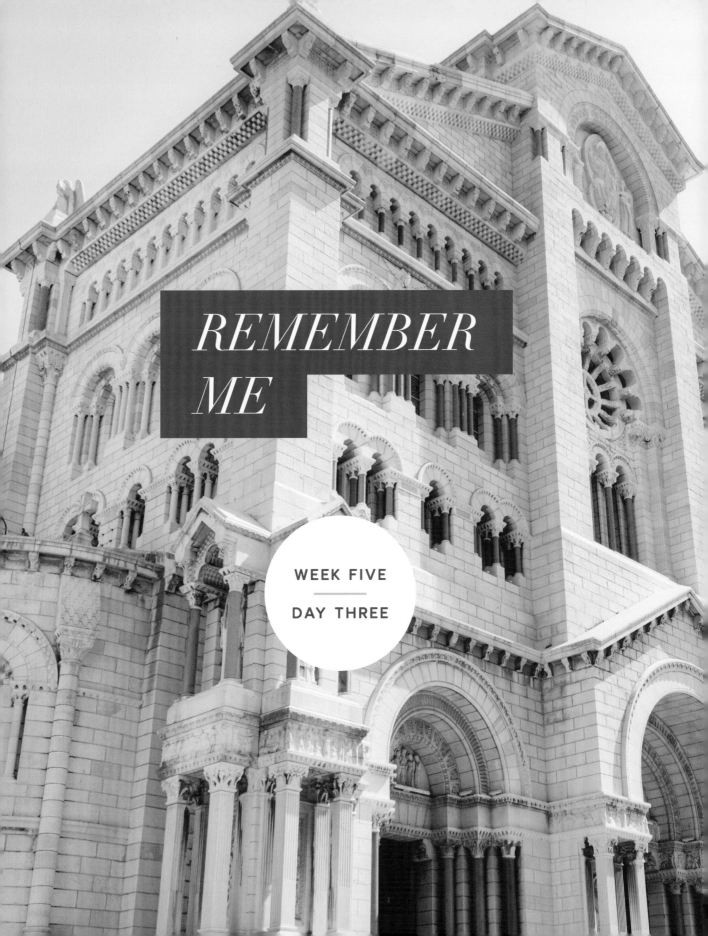

REMEMBER ME

WEEK FIVE

DAY THREE

NEHEMIAH 13

Nehemiah 12 ended in triumph. It seemed like the perfect end to the story. But it wasn't the end. If this were a movie, "twelve years later" would appear at the bottom of the screen, and the scene would shift. The bright and joyful celebration of chapter 12 would change into the bleak scene of chapter 13. In this scene we would see that the people that had signed their names to a covenant, had wandered away from the promises they had made. If we have studied chapter 9, we should not be surprised to know that the nation of Israel had failed again. But after studying the book of Nehemiah, we should also not be surprised to see that it is the Word of God that will begin another quest for revival and reformation in the life of Israel. In our lives as well, it is the Word of God and the Spirit of God that bring us back to the Lord. This section of Nehemiah reminds us of our constant need to return to the Lord. We are people that are prone to wander, and prone to forget, and it is the Word of God that draws us back to the Lord again and again.

Nehemiah returns to Jerusalem to find that things had fallen apart in many ways. Though the wall and the temple stood, the people had forgotten the covenant that they had made to worship, to be set apart, and to care for the house of the Lord. Tobiah is introduced back into the narrative, and we find that he has taken up residence in the house of God. The priest, Eliashib, was related to Tobiah and somehow allowed the idolatrous enemy of Israel to not only live in Israel but inside the temple. Sin had gotten so close that it had become comfortable. This was in many ways an illustration of spiritual truth as idolatry crept in because it was familiar. The same can easily happen in our lives. We must be on guard. We must be in God's Word so that we will be prepared to fight our own sin and the attacks of our enemy.

The people had also forsaken their pledge to keep the Sabbath. They had chosen work and enterprise over the worship of God. Though we are not under the Old Testament law anymore as New Testament believers, the principle of sabbath is still one that benefits us greatly. In a world that clamors for our attention, there is something sacred about time that is set aside for worship, for God's Word, and for fellowship with God's people. We have found ultimate sabbath rest in Jesus, and now we can adore Him by spending time with Him.

The last issue that Nehemiah addressed was that of intermarriage. Again, we must be reminded that this had nothing to do with nationalities and everything to do with a command for believers not to marry unbelievers. The Ammonites and Moabites were specifically named as some of the idolatrous nations that Israel had chosen to marry. But we know from our study of Scripture that God was ready and willing to extend mercy to those from these nations that would reject their idols and turn to the one living God. The book of Ruth is a beautiful example of a Moabite woman who was converted to Yahweh and then married to an Israelite man. Ruth would even be included in the genealogy of Jesus.

Throughout this final chapter we see a repeated prayer from Nehemiah. In verses 14, 22, and 31, he prays for God to remember him. We have seen throughout the book that Nehemiah was a man of fervent prayer. From his dedicated prayer time to the prayers that he prayed in turbulent moments, his life was characterized by prayer. As the book closes, we see him praying again. This is not the pompous prayer of a man looking for worldly recognition for his faithfulness. This is the humble prayer of a man who was well aware of his own weakness, but also of the strength and steadfast love of His God. It is interesting to note in verse 14 that the Hebrew word used to describe his good or faithful deeds is the word *Hesed*. This Hebrew word is one of the most prominent descriptions of God in the Old Testament. Nehemiah was praying that the faithful and steadfast love of God would help him to continue to be faithful and steadfast to God in return. May this be our prayer as well. May we never neglect our need to return again to the Lord. And may we praise Him for His steadfast love that seeks us out in the times that we are faithful and the times that we are unfaithful.

1 How does the book of Nehemiah and chapter 13 in particular point to the importance of God's Word in the life of the believer?

2 The people were prone to forget the covenant that they had made with the Lord and how He had been faithful. So often we are prone to forget the Lord as well. How can we intentionally remember the Lord?

3 The book of Nehemiah ends with another prayer of Nehemiah. We have seen Nehemiah spend extended time in prayer and also pray in moments of anxiety and fear. How does the prayer life of Nehemiah encourage you to cultivate your prayer life?

"MAY WE NEVER NEGLECT
OUR NEED TO RETURN
AGAIN TO THE LORD.

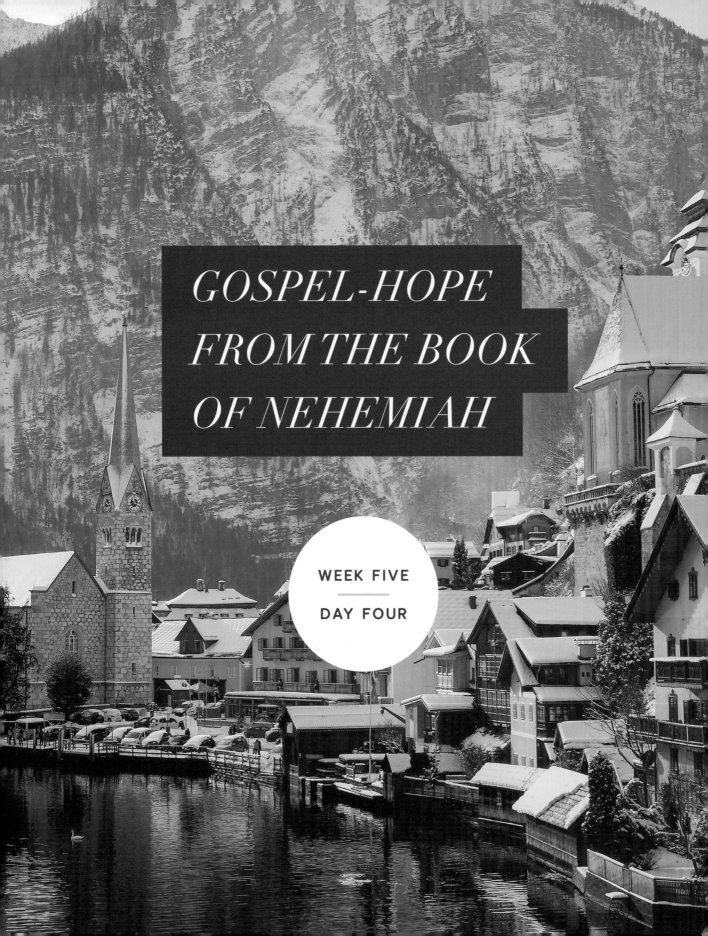

GOSPEL-HOPE FROM THE BOOK OF NEHEMIAH

WEEK FIVE
DAY FOUR

READ THE ENTIRE BOOK OF NEHEMIAH

As we come to the end of our study, go back and read the entire book of Nehemiah again. Don't be tempted to skip this step. It will be so helpful to read the story again now that you have studied the text deeper.

The book of Nehemiah is a book of yearning and a book of gospel-hope. It is a book that points us to our constant need for deliverance. It is a book that reminds us of our need for God's Word and the power of prayer. In the book of Nehemiah, God's people are called to arise and build, and God arises in faithfulness to walk with His people. But all of this points us over four centuries in the future to the answer to the promise that the people in Nehemiah's day longed for. On that day a star would arise over Bethlehem, and a King would arise from a manger bed. And now we as God's people are called to arise and build the kingdom here on earth.

The people in the book of Nehemiah returned to the promised land and waited for the promised King. They were joyful about rebuilt walls and the return from exile, but their hearts yearned for the coming on the Son of David who would fulfill the promise that they clung to. They were holding on to a promise that was made to David in 2 Samuel 7 that God would raise up a King from the line of David and establish the Davidic line forever. Jesus would be the fulfillment of that promise, and the people waited from the city of God for the Promised One. I can only imagine how their hearts yearned to see that promise fulfilled. They did not know when He would come, and their nation was riddled by sin and rebellion. They needed a deliverer, and Jesus was the One. Over and over we saw how Israel failed to keep their side of the covenant. They tried to be holy. They tried to follow the law. They tried, but they always failed, because no matter how hard they tried, they could never live up to God's standard. Yet even this was a picture of what was to come. Because one day the Messiah would come and He would keep the covenant that they could not keep. He would bring a new covenant that would be written on their hearts (Jeremiah 31:31-34, Ezekiel 37:26-28, Luke 22:20, Hebrews 8). Because though Nehemiah was a great leader, he could never transform the hearts of the people of Israel–only Christ could do that.

As the people ached for the Messiah and waited, they doubtless would have questioned. *Will He keep His promise? Will God do what He had said He would do?* I wonder if you have ever felt the same way. If you have ever found yourself in a season of waiting and struggle and wondered if God would be faithful to you. Or if you have ever felt like perhaps you had been passed by while God's blessing came to those around you. The book of Nehemiah is not the end of the story though; the story would continue with Jesus coming as the Promised One. Though it wasn't in the timing that the people had anticipated, Jesus came at just the right time (Romans 5:6). A season of waiting is not the end of your story. God was abundantly faithful to Jeremiah and the remnant that returned to Israel, and we can be assured that He will be faithful to us as well.

1 Write a summary of the book of Nehemiah.

2 Write out an outline of the book of Nehemiah. You can make it as simple or as thorough as you would like.

3 What are the biggest takeaways from the book of Nehemiah? How does this differ from what you thought when you first started the study?

HOWEVER, IN YOUR ABUNDANT COMPASSION, YOU DID NOT DESTROY THEM OR ABANDON THEM, FOR YOU ARE A GRACIOUS AND COMPASSIONATE GOD.

Nehemiah 9:31

WEEK FIVE REFLECTION

READ NEHEMIAH 11:1–13:31

Paraphrase the passage from this week.

_____

What did you observe from this week's text about God and His character?

_____

What does the passage teach about the condition of mankind and about yourself?

_____

How does this passage point to the gospel?

How should you respond to this passage? What is the personal application?

What specific action steps can you take this week to apply the passage?

JERUSALEM IN THE TIME OF NEHEMIAH

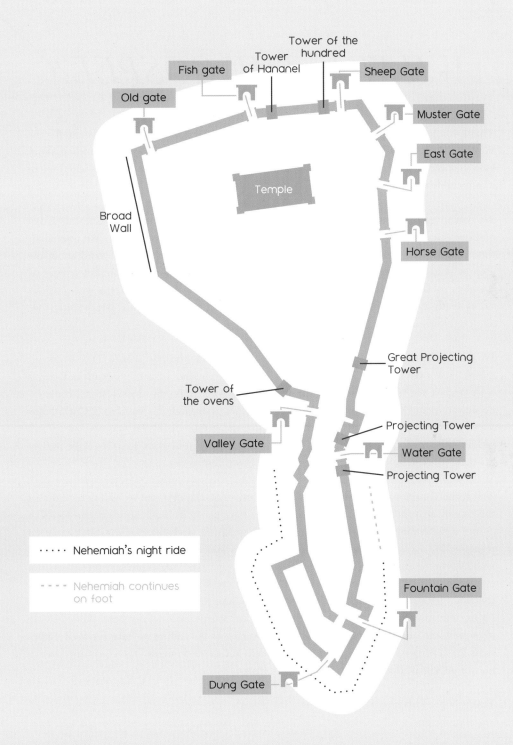

Fish gate

Tower of the hundred

Tower of Hananel

Sheep Gate

Old gate

Muster Gate

East Gate

Temple

Broad Wall

Horse Gate

Great Projecting Tower

Tower of the ovens

Projecting Tower

Valley Gate

Water Gate

Projecting Tower

Nehemiah's night ride

Nehemiah continues on foot

Fountain Gate

Dung Gate

WHAT IS THE GOSPEL?

Thank you for reading and enjoying this study with us! We are abundantly grateful for the Word of God, the instruction we glean from it, and the ever-growing understanding about God's character from it. We're also thankful that Scripture continually points to one thing in innumerable ways: the gospel.

We remember our brokenness when we read about the fall of Adam and Eve in the garden of Eden (Genesis 3), when sin entered into a perfect world and maimed it. We remember the necessity that something innocent must die to pay for our sin when we read about the atoning sacrifices in the Old Testament. We read that we have all sinned and fallen short of the glory of God (Romans 3:23), and that the penalty for our brokenness, the wages of our sin, is death (Romans 6:23). We all are in need of grace, mercy, and most importantly—we all need a Savior.

We consider the goodness of God when we realize that He did not plan to leave us in this dire state. We see His promise to buy us back from the clutches of sin and death in Genesis 3:15. And we see that promise accomplished with Jesus Christ on the cross. Jesus Christ knew no sin yet became sin so that we might become righteous through His sacrifice (2 Corinthians 5:21.) Jesus was tempted in every way that we are and lived sinlessly. He was reviled, yet still yielded Himself for our sake, that we may have life abundant in Him. Jesus lived the perfect life that we could not live and died the death that we deserved.

The gospel is profound yet simple. There are many mysteries in it that we can never exhaust this side of heaven, but there is still overwhelming weight to its implications in this life. The gospel is the telling of our sinfulness and God's goodness, and this gracious gift compels a response. We are saved by grace through faith (Ephesians 2:8-9), which means that we rest with faith in the grace that Jesus Christ displayed on the cross. We cannot save ourselves from our brokenness or do any amount of good works to merit God's favor, but we can have faith that what Jesus accomplished in His death, burial, and resurrection was more than enough for our salvation and our eternal delight. When we accept God, we are commanded to die to our self and our sinful desires and live a life worthy of the calling we have received (Ephesians 4:1). The gospel compels us to be sanctified, and in so doing, we are conformed to the likeness of Christ Himself.

This is hope. This is redemption. This is the gospel.

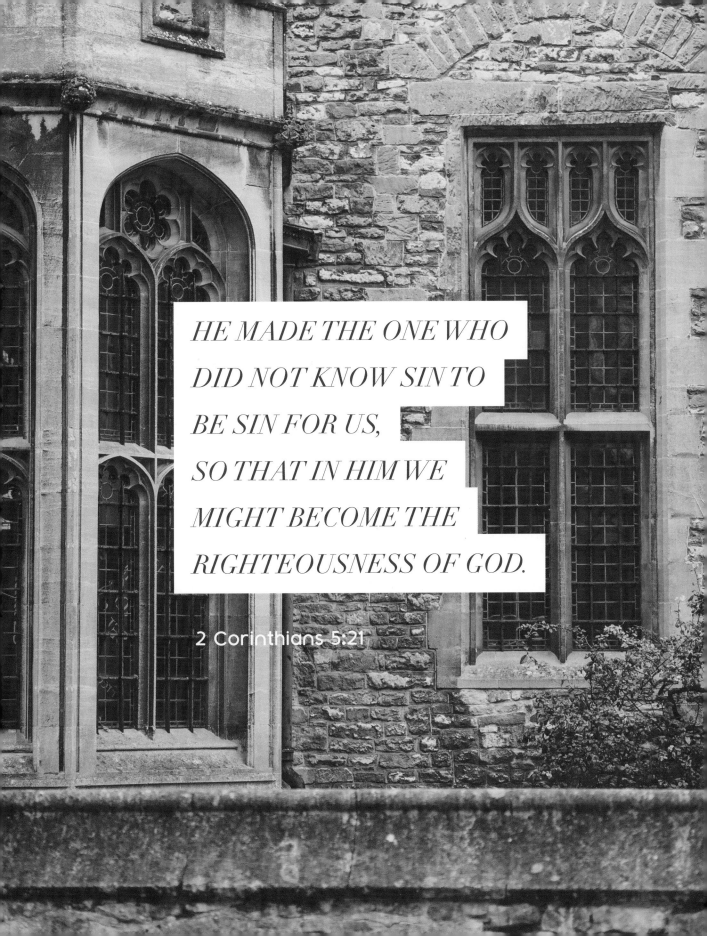

HE MADE THE ONE WHO DID NOT KNOW SIN TO BE SIN FOR US, SO THAT IN HIM WE MIGHT BECOME THE RIGHTEOUSNESS OF GOD.

2 Corinthians 5:21

FOR STUDYING GOD'S
WORD WITH US!

CONNECT WITH US:

@THEDAILYGRACECO
@KRISTINSCHMUCKER

CONTACT US:

INFO@THEDAILYGRACECO.COM

SHARE:

#THEDAILYGRACECO
#LAMPANDLIGHT

WEBSITE:

WWW.THEDAILYGRACECO.COM
